HIS GRACE IN THE MIDST OF TRAGEDY

HIS GRACE IN THE MIDST OF TRAGEDY

EDWARD LAPOINTE

ARPress

ILLUMINATING IDEAS
EMPOWERING VOICES

ARPress
45 Dan Road Suite 5
Canton, MA 02021

Hotline: 1(888) 821-0229
Fax: 1(508) 545-7580

Ordering Information:
Quantity sales. Special discounts are available on quantity purchases by corporations,associations, and others. For details, contact the publisher at the address above.

Printed in the United States of America.

ISBN-13:   Softcover   979-8-89389-209-3
              eBook   979-8-89389-210-9

Library of Congress Control Number: 2024905658

CONTENTS

INTRODUCTION

I finished the first draft of this manuscript in early 1991.

I attended a community college where I enrolled in a creative writing course. After my professor read my manuscript, he stated, "I would like to present this to a publisher." I agreed and gave him permission.

A bout a month later my professor came back to me and informed me that the publisher had gotten back to him. The answer was not what I wanted to hear. The publisher would not publish the book.

I asked, "Why? He answered, "the publisher said: there is no hope in it."

Those words resonated in my spirit. As I pondered those words, I realized that the publisher was right. There was no hope in it. Not only in the book, but in my life as well. The first draft ended with this sentence: "Little did I know that I would be back in the State Hospital in four years, to serve another four years.

The reason for being returned to the hospital this second time was for trying to pass a forged prescription for Percocet. An addicted family member said he would give me $200 to fill the prescription.

I was confined to the hospital and placed under the Psychiatric Security Review Board (PSRB). The PSRB patients were kept at Dutcher Hall, Connecticut Valley Hospital (CVH).

I will not go into detail about these four years, because my main focus will be on the tragedy. I just want to give you some background of what happened after the second and third times; after my first release.

After I was released the second time, I was still under the care of the PSRB; living in an apartment program. I was receiving Social Security disability and worked a part-time job as an auto-parts driver.

In December 1998, I was lying in my bed, it was very late, about 1 AM. I suddenly I had a thirst for God. I don't know how to explain it; I just wanted Jesus. I have always believed Jesus was the Savior, yet I did not know Him. I wanted to know Him.

I remembered that one of the third shift staff members was a born-again Christian. I called the office and asked him, "do you have any tapes?"

He said, "I have one in my car, I'll bring it over."

As I listened to the tape, the minister was speaking of divine healing. At this time, I had been seeing a doctor for a bad case of chronic bronchitis. So, I prayed; Lord heals my chronic bronchitis and mental illness. Immediately I could literally feel the healing power of God throughout my body. At that moment I was caught up in His love for me. This tangible supernatural love lasted five days. For the first time, I had found the hope that was missing, not only in my book, but more importantly; my life. That night I gave myself to the Lord. I have not been the same since.

It is difficult to get my point across about my salvation and third hospitalization without going into more detail. After my supernatural experience I believed my schizophrenia was supernaturally healed. I would not realize that it wasn't until a year later.

After my supernatural experience and salvation, I told everyone and anyone who would listen about it: Including my psychologist and psychiatrist.

About a year later I requested my psychiatrist to lower my medication. He lowered it to a dose that was below the recommended therapeutic dose.

For over a month I experienced no problems; that was until I decided to stop taking my medication altogether. I told no one about this.

I began to decompensate, having delusional thoughts, such as being a prophet. It all came to a climax when I destroyed my apartment; thinking it was full of dust mites. The police were called, and I was transported to CVH and hospitalized for four years.

You may be asking, where is there any hope in this? Well first; I am not finished yet. Also, salvation is in itself, all the hope we would ever need.

Four years after that hospitalization I went to court and was completely exonerated from State custody. That was 15 years ago. Five years ago, I was awarded VA service-connected disability; after 30 years of VA denials. I am now awaiting the VA decision for 24 years of retroactive benefits. I would call that a little hope!

"YES" I am taking my medications; I realize that God has chosen that method to keep me well.

Now that I have revealed the hope, I will speak about the tragedy that occurred in my and my family's life.

BACKROUND

Before I was drafted into the Marines in 1969, I had attended high school and worked a full or part-time job. I would have been considered a normal young adult with no signs of a psychiatric disorder.

In the Marines I was promoted to the rank of Lance Cpl. in a relatively short period of time; held a secret clearance and qualified as a sharpshooter twice and expert once with a rifle. I also qualified as a marksman with a pistol.

In October 1970 I received orders to go to Okinawa. This is where my alcohol and drug use immensely increased; I was using drugs and alcohol to help me cope. Something in me was beginning to change; I don't even know how to explain it. A few months before I was to come home, I went absent without leave for three days. As punishment I was demoted to the rank of Pfc.

Upon returning home I was honorably discharged.

I returned to my former place of employment where I worked for a couple of months and was fired for missing work. This routine and result followed me at every place of employment.

I met my wife Patty in early 1972; It was love at first sight for both of us. A few months later we learned she was pregnant; we decided to marry in September 1972.

In March 1973 our son Michael was born and in July 1974 our daughter Rene was born.

During these first few years of our marriage, I went from job to job. In November 1975 I was hired by a gun manufacture, where I worked for a year until the tragedy. This was my longest period of employment since my honorable discharge from the Marines four years earlier.

During those four years I was becoming more and more aggressive. My drinking and drug use increased; I was constantly getting into bar fights and arguments. These signs of my schizophrenia were not of who I used to be. I felt like there was something missing in my spirit. I tried to fill it with drugs and alcohol and when those did not work, I tried to fill it with other women. None of these desires worked.

I believe the Bible says: that God puts a void in everyone's heart (spirit) that can only be filled with the Spirit of God. I can attest to this today because He has come to fill that void.

THE SHOOTING

It was November 18, 1976; I had been struggling with confusion and growing paranoia for going on a week. This day I was going to change the course of my life and the lives of many others and end the life of the only person who had ever shown me unconditional love.

I had no previous knowledge of the mental disorder that I would be diagnosed with in just a few days: Paranoid Schizophrenia.

Since the previous week I was having numerous delusions, and the paranoia was becoming unbearable. So much so, that at work I asked my foreman, George, a Viet Nam Marine veteran, "How long did it take you to get over almost being killed in combat."

"You get over it. Why do you ask?"

"I was almost shot last night." I replied.

I walked out of his office and over to the parts inspector, Sal, I said, "Three guys from the mafia came into the Fireside Cafe last night. One of them almost shot me. When it was over the guy in charge shook my hand."

"You're lucky he shook your hand instead of giving you a kiss on the right cheek." He replied.

I went to my machine but was having a difficult time concentrating. Al, one of my coworkers came over; I asked him, "Have you ever felt like a computer?"

"Feel like a computer, what do you mean?"

"I feel like a computer, that I'm being programmed."

"You feel like that, Ted?"

"Yes."

He looked at me kind of funny, and then walked away.

A while later, Dave, another coworker, came over and said, "Maybe you should go to Florida till things cool off."

"What the hell is he talking about?!" I asked myself.

During break, while Dave and I were walking through the shop, I asked him, "Am I dead?!"

"You're still walking."

That answer set my thoughts running wild.

I went into the cafeteria, while I was sitting at a table, another coworker, Bob, came over and sat down; Bob supposedly has family in the mob. He said, "They only want what is right."

"Where is all this coming from?" I asked myself.

I must have gone into a blackout, because the next thing I remember was Dave at the table. "Do you want a ride home?" He asked.

I thought if I went with him, I would be killed. In fear I answered, "I'll call my wife!"

I walked to the door that led to the parking lot, I opened the door, parked by the door was my usual ride home, waiting for me. I remember getting into the car, which was all I recall till they dropped me off at the beginning of my street.

The walk from there to my house seemed like the longest walk of my life. I remember looking over my shoulder the entire way.

When I got to my door I unlocked it, the lights were all off, and Patty was in bed. I was terrified and turned all the lights in the house on.

"Ted why are you turning all the lights on?" Patty asked,

"I don't know." I replied.

I got undressed and got into bed.

Patty got out of bed; she turned off the lights and returned to bed.

In bed, I said to Patty, "Their going to kill me!"

"Why, are you sleeping with someone's wife?"

"No."

"Ted, I think you're having a nervous breakdown."

"Well, wouldn't you be nervous if you were going to be killed?"

The next think I knew it was morning., The kids were up and running around.

That morning the blackouts and lapses of time continued. At one point I was sitting on the end of our bed, Patty came in.

"Do you know Dave," I knew Patty knew him because we double dated one time.

"Yes"

"He screwed me in the ass!"

"Why didn't you tell me, Ted?"

"That didn't happen; why did I say that?"

3

I had no recollection of time, I remember walking around the house and being in one room and then another, not remembering going from one to the other.

I remember leaning on the top of the dryer and saying, "Something is going to happen, but I don't know what it is!"

It must have become time for me to go to work, because Patty asked, "Are you going to get ready for work?"

"If I go to work something is going to happen."

"OK." She answered.

She called my work, I heard her say to my foreman, "Ted won't be in tonight."

He must have asked her what was wrong with me.

"I don't know. I am trying to find out." She replied and hung up.

A little while later Patty came to me with one of our small Marijuana pipes,

"Here smoke this." She said. I guess she thought it might relax me and calm me down, but it just increased the paranoia.

Around 5pm Patty asked, "Ted, it is almost time for me to go to school. Do you want me to bring the kids to my mothers, or will you watch them?"

She was going to night school to get her GED. Her mother would watch the kids when she went.

"You can't go. If you go something is going to happen."

"Ted, if I don't go, I will have to start the school over from the beginning."

"You can't go; something will happen if you go." I repeated.

"Ted, what will happen?"

"I don't know, but something will happen if you go."

She called her mom and told her she was staying home.

The phone rang, Patty answered it. "Your brother Johnny from Maine wants to speak to you."

I got on the phone; I said, "So you're the one who is going to do it! Well come right ahead and try!" I hung up.

I learned later that he called to ask if he could come to our home for Thanksgiving dinner with my mother; she was coming for Thanksgiving.

He must have called our mother. Because a few minutes later the phone rang.

Patty answered, "Your mom wants to speak to you."

I took the phone, "My mother asked, "Ted, are you high?"

"Yea, I am high on life!"

She said, "I have to go pick up your brother Charlie from the airport. I will speak with you later." She hung up.

I had this penetrating feeling, "I have to speak with my mother." I tried to call her back, but she had left to pick up my brother Charlie at the airport. He was coming home on leave from the Navy, but I thought she was picking up his body and bringing him home.

I felt I had to see my mother; I became so obsessed about it that I told Patty, "Get the kids ready were going to my mothers." (This was the first huge mistake).

"Your mother is not home, Ted." She replied.

I insisted, she finally agreed, and got the kids ready.

I began to smell a foul odor; it was an odor I had never smelled before, and I have never smelled it again since that day. It was the worse odor I have ever smelled. Looking back; I now believe it was the smell of death.

As we got into Patty's wagon, the smell was driving crazy! Even though outside it was a cold evening, I opened my window, hoping to expel that smell.

We stopped at the corner to buy gas; we were then on our way.

The funny thing is my mother had just moved into a new apartment. I had only been there once, and then, I drove with someone else. I have a difficult time remembering my way somewhere when I'm not the one driving. So, I really had no idea if I could find her apartment, especially in the dark.

To get to Naugatuck, where my mom lived, we had to drive through New Haven.

Somehow, we came to Yale New Haven Hospital, which was not on the direct route that we needed to go. As we were driving by the hospital I asked Patty, "Should I go in?"

"It's up to you." She replied.

Something told me, "Don't go in." (The second huge mistake).

As I was driving, I began to believe we were being followed. I made the decision to drive through Shelton to stop at a lifelong family friend. Just when we were going to pull up in front of their house I saw a vehicle in my rear-view mirror, this vehicle had made the last three turns that I had. I believed he might be following us. We were less than a block away from our friend's home, I turned left and parked on the side of the street. The vehicle behind us went by, not making the turn. I made the decision not to go to our friend's home. (This was the third mistake).

I drove back to Rout 8 North heading to Naugatuck, having to go by Beacon Falls, a town where ten years ago my mom lived when she was married to my stepfather. I had this thought, "My mom is at her old house." I turned right and drove to her old house.

As we reached the house, Patty said, "Oh, your mom's old house."

I was able to see a person sitting at the dining room window. I thought it was my stepfather, that is where he always sat.

I decided not to drive into the driveway. I turned left and drove back to Route 8.

When we reached Naugatuck, we drove around the area where I thought my mom lived. After a long while of driving around, I pulled into an apartment complex and parked in front of an apartment building where I believed she lived, but deep inside I knew I actually had no idea where I was.

I asked Patty, "Do you want to come in?"

"I can't go in like this." she answered.

I looked to my left, I saw a man and a woman walking, I was overcome with terror; I thought it was Johnny, my brother. The thought returned, "I know he wants to kill me!"

I decided to drive back towards home.

We drove past the exit to our home and continued to Branford, my hometown, where my father still lived. We came to a McDonalds.

Patty said, "The kids haven't eaten, and they need to use the bathroom."

I pulled in and parked.

I brought the kids inside and into the restroom. First Michael went, then Rene. I went when they were finished, as I was urinating, I looked into the toilet, my urine was streaming out blood. Not just the color of blood, it was blood in a stream as urine.

When I finished, I bought the kids a meal, and we went back to the car.

In the car I said to Patty, "My urine was blood."

While the kids were eating, Michael said something I will never forget. He said, "Mommy is going to die." I will never know until that day when I meet my Lord Jesus if Michael really said that.

I turned to Patty, "Did you hear what he said?!"

"Yes." Let's go home."

Five hours passed since we left the house. During the time we were gone my father in-law, Jerome, went to our home and let himself in, he has a key. While he was there my mother and Charlie also arrived. They all sensed something was seriously wrong with the way I was behaving. They talked about taking my guns out of the house but decided against it. (Another huge mistake that could have stopped what was about to happen).

We were only home a few minutes when Jerome and Jerry, my brother in-law, came in. I was standing by a cabinet in the dining room looking at a book; I think it was a phone book. Jerry walked over to me,

"What do you want me to do, eat it!?" I asked him sarcastically. He just looked at me. I then asked Jerome, "How do you like our new color TV?" The reason this question didn't make any sense, is that it is a black and white TV. Our color TV went, my father gave us the black and white to use.

I went into the kitchen; Patty was boiling water for coffee. I put my arms around her, and we were hugging. I later learned that while we were hugging, Jerome came into the kitchen doorway, Patty motioned to him that everything was okay. I never saw them leave the house.

The next place I found myself, not remembering going there, was lying on the couch. The TV was on, but I don't remember hearing it. I didn't see Patty coming over to me. She lied down on top of me; a terror I can never express with words shot thru me. I pushed Patty off of me, I began saying over and over again, "Someone is in the house! Someone is in the house!" I went into the dining room where my guns were hanging on the gun rack. I took down the shotgun and took my shells from the rack; there were only two shotgun shells; there were no rounds for my rifle. Having my guns and only two shells is another strange coincidence, if there is such a thing as coincidence. Two weeks before I had lent my guns and shells to Dave, my coworker, to use. I had just gotten them back a few days ago. When I lent them to him there was a full box of shogun shells and three high powered rounds for my rifle. When he returned the guns, he gave me just the two shotgun shells.

I loaded the two shells into the shotgun, Patty was looking at me in disbelieve. I could see the fear and confusion on her face.

I said, "Patty, check the house, someone is in the house!"

"Ted, no one is in the house."

I said it again, "Someone is in this house!"

"I'll check the house." She replied.

The next thing I saw is Patty coming around the corner from the hallway into the living room. I was startled and aimed the gun at her. I instantly realized it was her and lowered the gun.

"Ted, no one is in the house. Do you think I am going to kill you?!"

I shook my head, "No"

As I began to unload the gun, I had this delusion that Dave was in the hallway with his gun, he owned a 45 caliber pistol. I put the shells back in the gun.

Patty was sitting at the dining room table, to the left of me. She had her head in her hands.

She must have been thinking, "What in the hell is going on!

I must have gone into another blackout. I didn't see Patty get up from the table and go to the living room window, maybe she thought someone was outside. The next think I remember is coming out of the blackout, at the same instant there was this scream in my head that screamed, "NOW!" I saw someone backing away from the living room window, I fired, and it was Patty.

At the same instant I fired I knew it was Patty, but it was too late, I couldn't bring it back.

I screamed, "GOD! GOD!"

I walked to the other side of the dining room by the windows. I took the gun and put the barrel against the right back side of my head. It was difficult to hold the gun and reach the trigger with my thumb. I was finally able to pull the trigger. It didn't go off. I looked at the gun; the slide for the pump action had slid down; the gun won't fire with the slide down. I pulled the slide up. This time I put the barrel under my chin. When I pulled the trigger, it fired.

The blow only blacked me out for a second, I was still standing there. I was in total disbelieve.

"How could I be alive?"

I walked over to the gun rack; I searched for more shells, there were none. I remember looking up at the ceiling and seeing all the shot holes, I had this delusion that Dave put feathers in my shell, and that was the reason I wasn't dead.

The real reason I was still alive is that the barrel was too long, my father had told me later. I had to hold my head all the way back to get the barrel under my chin. The blast went in thru my bottom jaw and out my mouth. If I would have been able to hold my head lower, it would have killed me instantly. Regardless of that, I realized I had been gravely wounded; I knew if I waited long enough, I would bleed to death.

I began walking around and around the dining room table making weird sounds.

The phone rang, I answered it, and it was my mother in-law.

She asked, "Can I speak with Patty?"

"She's gone."

"Where did she go?"

"She is dead."

I was making these terrible moans due to the pain that was beginning to come on, the shock was wearing off. I hung up the phone.

As I continued to walk around the table, I heard my son calling.

"Mommy! Mommy!"

I walked to the kitchen doorway where I could see him standing in their bedroom doorway. His sister was standing behind him.

"Put your sister in her crib and go to bed and stay in your room."

My daughter did not see me, but my son did, I could see the fear on his face. He did as I told him and went into his room.

The phone rang again, I answered it, and it was my mother in-law again.

"What happened, Ted?"

"There is a strange man in the house."

"Who, Ted?"

"Me."

"Where did you shoot yourself?"

"In the face."

"Do you want help?"

"No."

"Call for Jerome if you want help."

I hung up the phone.

I went and lay with Patty, my head on her lap. I kept repeating, "Almost Patty, almost. I'll be with you soon."

The phone rang again. I answered it. It was my brother Charlie, he said, "Hi Ted."

"I can't talk now."

I dropped the receiver on the floor and went back to lay with Patty.

I don't know how much time went by when the phone started making a very weird sound. I got up and walked over to the phone. I picked up the receiver.

I said, "Hello."

A man answered, "This is Sgt. so and so, may I speak to your wife?"

"She is gone."

"Her car is in the driveway."

"She is gone." I repeated.

"Where are the children?"

"They are in bed."

I dropped the receiver. I went back to lay with Patty.

I do not remember how much time had gone by, but it was a while. I began getting the feeling of pins and needles throughout my body. I knew I had lost a lot of blood and it wouldn't long before I would black out.

There was a loud knock on the back door. I heard my mother calling my name. "Teddy! Teddy!"

"Mom! Mom!" I yelled back.

"Let us help you, Ted."

I went to stand up but didn't have the strength; I crawled to the back door. There were three locks on the door; I unlocked them one at a time. I expected to be shot as soon as I opened the door. I opened the door, stepped back, my eyes closed. My mother wrapped her arms around me to protect me. An officer sat me in a kitchen chair; he put hand cuffs on me.

He asked me "Why did you shoot your wife?"

I started shaking my hands and making strange groans.

I heard my mom say, "Dear Jesus, Mary and Joseph!"

A couple of minutes later I was being carried out of the house; I don't remember anything else until I was in Yale New Haven Hospital.

I am not exactly sure, but I believe from the time I shot myself to the time I opened the door, was about four hours. My mother had to drive from Naugatuck and that alone is an hour drive.

The swat team was outside the entire time. The reason they didn't barge in was because of our children's' safety. I guess they couldn't see me thru the window, or they may have taken a shot.

My dad asked me sometime later why it took me so long to shoot myself? The upstairs neighbor stated it was a half an hour between shots. I must have been in another blackout; to me it seemed like only a few seconds.

THE HOSPITAL

I have no recollection of anything after they were taking me out of the house.

Years later my father in-law told me, "You looked like a ghost."

The first remembrance I have of the hospital is coming conscious in the Yale ER, I felt someone pumping on my chest.

I have no explanations for what happened next. I ejaculated.

Someone said, "It must feel good to be reborn." That just might be the explanation.

I began growling and trying to sit up. They pushed me down.

Someone asked, "What does he think he is? An animal!"

I opened my eyes; there were a number of people standing around me. I saw this one man who was dressed in a suit; I figured he was either a detective or a doctor. I looked at him, and I gave him the thumb up sign; I have no idea why.

Someone said, "We have to get him to surgery."

I fell into unconsciousness again.

I became conscious again in the operating room.

I heard someone ask, "What happened to him?"

"He tried to blow his head off!" Someone replied.

As I was about to go unconscious from the anesthesia, I saw two demons leave me, they seemed to come out from the top of my head. I believe they were murdering, and suicidal demons. They were hideous creatures. I then saw, what I believe to be the angel of the Lord who I believe cast the two demons from me. All I saw was his head, he had a beard and looked very strong, he just looked at me. Then I went unconscious.

I do not know how long I had been in the ICU; the first memory I have of it was when I heard my mom's voice say, "Ted."

I could barely open my eyes; I saw tubes and machines around me.

"It's good to see your heartbeat."

I fell back to sleep.

Sometime later my dad and stepmother, Betty, came in.

My dad said, "Ted, you were in surgery for eight hours. Your bottom lip didn't take; they want to take you down in the morning to do a graft. Is that alright with you?"

I nodded my head, "Yes."

I had no sense of time; and I have no recollection of going to surgery the next morning.

At some point, two doctors came in.

One asked, "Can you look at this chart? We want to check your vision."

I nodded my head, "Yes."

They gave me a pen; I was unable to look where I was writing, one of them directed my hand to the paper. They pointed to the letters on the chart; I wrote what I saw on the paper. One of them said, "Your vision is perfect."

I remember a nurse at the foot of my bed; as she was touching my left foot, she asked, "Can you feel that?"

I felt a warm sensation in my foot.

I nodded my head, "Yes."

"That's your pain medication going in threw an IV in your foot." She stated.

I had no knowledge of whether it was day or night, or if I had been there hours or days. I was sleeping almost all the time.

At some point I began thinking about God, which I hadn't done since I was a child. I had this overwhelming desire to be like Christ, I stretched out my arms and put my right foot over my left. The nurse came over and uncrossed my feet. I crossed them again, again she uncrossed them and said, "You're going to pull out your IV." I crossed them again, again she uncrossed them, I crossed them again. She must have become tired, she walked away.

My dad and Betty came to see me. I motioned with my hand that I wanted to write.

He said to the nurse, "He wants to write something." She gave me a pen and paper.

I wrote, "I love you."

"We love you, too."

Years later I was speaking with Betty about my time in ICU.

She said, "I have never seen anyone's face so swollen; it was the size of a volleyball."

At some point, my mom came again; while she was there, three nurses from the burn unit came in. They walked to my bedside and looked at me. These were the nurses I had when I was in the burn unit, two years before. I was burned in a factory accident; I had first, second and third degree burns that covered 60 percent of my body. I was not a newcomer to pain.

My dad and stepmother came to that point in time I had only opened my eyes a few times, but this day I tried. I could barely see, but I noticed that my dad had a suit and tie on. I thought to myself, "They must have had the funeral for Patty," because my dad only wears a suit and tie for weddings and funerals.

About two weeks went by, although I was unaware of how long I was there.

I was resting, when this guy in the bed next to me began yelling and yelling, he was driving me up the wall, I kept turning my head from side to side. I could not stand listening to him.

The nurse came over to the side of my bed.

"Ted, do you want to be moved downstairs."

I nodded, "Yes."

I was moved downstairs to a private room; I do not remember the actual move.

When I awoke, I looked around, there was a police officer sitting in the room with me. I was told the police were there because my brother in-laws had made threats against my life.

I was becoming more alert; I began staying awake for longer periods of time; it was about this time that I realized they had performed a tracheotomy on me. Every so often a nurse would come in and suction out my lungs by placing a suction tube down through the tube in my throat, all the way to the bottom of my lungs. There was little discomfort from it; I also had a feeding tube in my nostril, with which I was fed.

I began getting out of bed from time to time and spent time sitting in a chair.

One day the nurse was feeding me threw the feeding tube. The liquid meal kept backing up into my throat, I began to choke. I stopped her and wrote on a piece of paper, "It's coming back up."

They brought in an X-ray machine; they took pictures of my stomach, which showed the tube had moved up and out of my stomach. The doctor came in; pushed the tube back in where it belonged. I had no more problems with the feeding tube after that.

Three times a day a respiratory therapist came in and hooked up a vaporizer machine. I would inhale a medicated vapor threw a mouth and nose mask for ten minutes, or until the medicine in a small vile attached to the base of the mask was used up.

This would help loosen up the congestion in my lungs. When the treatment was over, the therapist would firmly pound on all areas of my back. When he would stop, I would sit up, and commence coughing; bringing up the mucus in my lungs, the nurse would finish the treatment by suctioning out my lungs.

One day, after a breathing treatment, I began my coughing, this time it was really bad. The mucus was streaming from my mouth.

The nurse said, "Ted, let me suction you out."

I refused to let her, I wanted to suffer.

The respiratory therapist said to her, "Let him be for a few minutes."

The coughing continued for a good ten minutes. When it finally stopped, I let her suction me out.

They had taken an X-ray of my lungs, and through my mom I learned they found a spot on one of my lungs; this was the reason for the breathing treatments, to loosen up the spot, so I could cough it up.

While my mother was visiting one afternoon, I began coughing; when I stopped, my mom saw something protruding out of the opening in the trake. She took a tissue and pulled out a nasty red clot.

She said, "It has finally come up, Ted."

The police who were assigned to watch me; sat in my room with me, except for one, he sat in the hallway with the door open.

On one afternoon I was sitting in my chair, I could no longer resist my curiosity. I wanted to see the damage I had done to my face. There was a mirror over by a sink in the corner of the room. I walked over, looked at myself. This may sound strange, but I thought I looked just like porky pig. I actually had a little chuckle at myself.

I also realized what a remarkable job the surgeons had done, considering what little was left for them to work with. I had thought it would be much worse.

One evening I was lying in bed with my back to the door, the evening news was on the TV. The officer was speaking with someone when the news announcer said, "The State Police are still investigating the murder and suicide attempt of a New Haven woman and her husband." The officer and the person he were speaking with stopped talking. I knew they were wandering if I heard it. I just laid there like I didn't hear anything.

There were three primary nurses who cared for me, but Mary was my favorite. She took excellent care of me. She would come in first thing every morning and check my face, to see if there were any stitches coming out. If there were, she would take tweezers and carefully remove them.

One particular morning she came in and asked, "Do you want to take a bath and have a shave?"

I nodded my head, "Yes."

The closest thing I had to a bath, was a sponge bath.

I remember my first sponge bath; it was the day after I came down from ICU. Mary gave it to me; I knew I stunk, that overwhelming odor of dried blood. When she was washing me, I could see her wrinkle her nose from the odor coming off me. When I came into the hospital I must have been covered with blood from head to toe.

Mary walked me into the shower room, where she ran the bath water. I took off my hospital gown and climbed into the tub. The water was nice and warm.

I was ready to wash myself, but Mary said, "Lay back."

I laid back, Mary soaked the face cloth and held it over my chest and slowly squeezed

water onto my chest. Then working her way down to my private area. Even though it felt good to have this affectionate touch I could not comprehend how someone could show love to me, after what I had done. She soaped up the cloth and washed me neck to feet. She then shampooed my hair.

After the bath I got out of the tub, she brought me a razor and shaving cream.

The officer came to watch me and to make sure I didn't try to cut myself.

I thought to myself, "You don't have to worry, if my 12 gauge didn't accomplish it, this razor sure won't." I carefully shaved my chin, in and out of all the crevices where the surgeons' stitched layers of skin together.

One afternoon three doctors came in, one of them, was Dr. Hart.

She said, "It is time for the feeding tube to come out. How do you feel about that?"

"How will I eat?" I wrote.

"We will give you a liquid supplement."

"That won't be enough." I wrote.

"Then we will leave it in for a while longer."

One of the other doctors practically yelled at her.

"It has to be removed!" He said.

As they pulled the tube out it felt very uncomfortable. I began to cry, not from the discomfort. I cried because I didn't think I would have enough food intake.

From that day on I began to drink supplements and soup, and shortly after I upgraded to puree meals. They were not very appetizing.

One evening my mom came to visit with me, as we sat together, she looked at me.

She asked, "Ted, do you remember what happened?"

I nodded my head, "Yes." On a paper I wrote, "Patty died."

"Was it premeditated?"

I turned my head from side to side, "No."

"I didn't think so."

I wrote, "It's a mortal sin."

I began crying. This was the mentality I had about the judgment of God, learned from my childhood in the catholic environment. It was not until 22 years later when I read the word of God for myself and learned that Jesus paid the price for all my sins not just some of them. The Word says the only unforgivable sin is blasphemy of the Holy Spirit.

That same evening while my mom was still there, my dad and stepmother came in. As we all sat together my dad asked, "Can you explain on paper what happened?"

I began writing the sequence of events that led up to the shooting.

I wrote how I was in the Fireside Cafe two nights before the shooting. I was with Linda a girl I had met in the Cafe, and a friend I hung around and drank with. Linda and I sat at a table with another couple I did not know, but Linda knew them. My friend, Fred, sat at the bar. Three men came in, whom I had never seen before. One stood alongside Fred, one stood at the far end of the bar and the third, he was in charge, stood between the other two.

It was just a couple of minutes after they entered the bar, when I heard Fred say, "No! No!"

I turned around and faced Fred and the man alongside him.

"Fred, what's wrong?" I asked.

He put his hand out and exclaimed.

"Ted, don't do anything!"

I looked at the guy who I knew was in charge.

"Fred is my friend; I want to know what is going on."

He stood there, not saying a word.

I turned back to Fred. "What do you think, Fred?"

I stood up and noticed the guy at the far end of the bar pull out a gun. The guy in charge put his arms out and stepped between me and the guy with the gun. I turned to the guy sitting at my table and exclaimed. "Did you see that guy jump in between my shit!"

He looked at me moving his eyes for me to look behind me. I turned around, the guy in charge was standing less than a foot in front of me, and he had his hand in his leather jacket as if he was ready to pull a weapon. I stood ready, if he goes to pull out a weapon, I was close enough to grab hold of him before he could pull it all the way out. It seemed like we stood there for an hour. He then slowly pulled out his hand; he reached out to shake my hand.

I then heard the guy standing alongside Fred, say to Fred

"Your friend just saved your life."

The guy in charge said to me.

"We just came in for a pack of smokes. I'll buy you a beer."

He turned to the guy at the far end of the bar.

"Put that thing away, and don't take it out again!"

As they were walking out the guy that was at the end of the bar stared at me as he was walking by, I could see it in his eyes, he wanted to murder me and he would have, if the one in charge hadn't stopped him. I have never seen such evil in a man's eyes.

I continued to write, and explain how I believed they were Mafia, how I began to think, these guys were going to wait till another time and finish what they came in to do. Not remembering it was Fred they came in for, not me. My parents were having a difficult time understanding everything I was writing.

"They accomplished what they wanted to do." My mom said out loud.

My dad, on the other hand believed the psychosis and all the events were caused due to drug use. This hurt me intensely; I began to cry and wrote.

"I don't understand why you didn't just let me die!"

My dad grabbed the paper and crumbled it up.

He then asked, "Why didn't you finish yourself off?"

"I couldn't find any more shells."

They could see these questions were taking a lot out of me.

My mom said, "We will leave and let you rest, we will see you tomorrow."

One evening I was sitting up in bed and this guy walked in and asked the officer who was sitting in the room with me.

"Is this the guy that tried to blow his head off?"

The officer did not answer him.

I gave that guy such an angry stare. As he looked at me, I could see the fear my stare put in him. As he was walking out, he kept turning back to look at me, I kept that stare on him till he was out of site. I never saw him again.

One afternoon my nurse, Mary asked me, "Would you like to take a walk down the hallway?"

I nodded, "Yes."

Mary and the officer walked me to the end of the hallway where there was a window that overlooked the street and parking lot.

"It's cold out, but the sun is out. "Would you like to look out the window?" She asked.

I looked out at the street and parking lot, I saw this man in a red leather jacket, he had the same color hair and jacket the guy in the bar had. A feeling of terror came over me. I turned from the window, looked at Mary and shook my head, "no!"

I could see she saw the fear in my face. "That's okay; let's go back to the room."

One evening when my parents and stepmother were visiting, a man came in; he introduced himself as a detective.

He then stated, "You are charged with the murder of your wife." He read me my rights and asked, "Do you wish to make a statement?"

I wrote, "What degree?"

"First."

I wrote, "I have nothing to say."

"Have a nice evening." He left.

One afternoon as I was sitting in my chair, one of the nurses came in, I later learned she was a police officer, and she always monitored my mail and reading things I wrote.

That was one of the reasons my family took anything I wrote about the shooting home, they also were trying to make some sense out of the things I wrote.

"You have a letter." She said. She was about four feet from me; she threw the letter at me angrily.

I tried to catch the letter; I broke into tears. I opened the letter; it was from my sister, Beverly.

She stood there while I was reading the letter.

"Can I read it?" She asked.

I gave her the letter. She read it, when she finished, she gave it back to me. I could see she felt bad. She thought it was from a girlfriend.

One morning Mary came in, she sat down on the bed next to me. She had a Q tip in her hand. She wrapped tape around and around one end of the Q tip. When she had wrapped enough tape around it, she cut it so that it was about ¾ 's of inch long. She leaned forward and pushed it into the opening in my trake.

She then said, "Ted, I want you to talk."

I thought for a moment, and then said, "I don't know if I can."

She smiled. Another nurse came into the room.

Mary said, "Ted, ask Carol, what's happening?"

"What's happening," I asked. The three of us started to laugh.

Later that same day my stepmother came to visit me. I was sitting in my chair when she came in and sat down. I looked over at her.

I said, "Hi Bet."

She looked at me with disbelieve, then she smiled.

"Hi, when did this happen?"

"A few hours ago." I answered.

One evening both my parents and my stepmother came to visit. We talked for a few minutes.

My dad asked, "We would like to know if you will speak to a psychiatrist here at the hospital? Would you mind talking to him about what happened?"

"I will, but I wouldn't know where to start."

"He'll ask you questions, and you answer the best you can. Just tell the truth, Ted." My mom said.

The next morning a man came to see me. He introduced himself as Dr. Walters one of the staff psychiatrists here at the hospital.

"Would you like to talk about what happened?"

"I don't know where to start."

"Start wherever you want to."

I told him the whole story of the events prior to, and the shooting itself.

When I finished, he asked, "Would you be willing to speak with the senior psychiatrist?"

"Yes." I answered.

"Dr. VanDyke will stop in to see you in a day or two."

That evening my brother Johnny, who drove down from Maine, came to visit. After we said our hello's, he said. "Ted, I spoke with some people I know, they have connections, and they told me there are no contracts put out on you."

"At this point I couldn't care less if there is or not." I replied.

The next day Dr. VanDyke came in, he introduced himself.

"Could you tell me what you told Dr. Walters yesterday?"

I told him the entire story.

When I finished, he asked, "How are you sleeping?"

"I am having real bad dreams."

"I'll order some medication to help you sleep; it will help with the paranoia, too. I will stop in again in a day or two."

The medication he ordered for me was a major tranquilizer named Trilafon; I was to take it 3 times a day.

December 14th, my birthday, came. My parents and stepmother came to visit. While they were there Mary brought in a small birthday cake. Everyone wished me happy birthday. I had a difficult time eating the cake, when I tried to chew it would fall out of my mouth. You have to remember, most of my left and bottom jawbone were missing and most of my teeth were missing and the ones I had were pushed back into place to try and save them. This was the first solid food I had. I have been eating puree food and liquids only.

It was a few days since Dr. VanDyke ordered the medication. He stopped in to see if it was helping with my bad dreams and sleep.

I said to him, "I have been getting severe headaches, could the medication be causing them?"

"I don't think so, but I'll look into it, and I will be back later today to let you know."

Later that afternoon Dr. VanDyke returned.

"The medication can have that side effect, so I am discontinuing it today."

I never asked him why, but after he discontinued that medication, he never ordered me anything else.

The next morning Mary came in.

"We have to move you to another room; you will be with two other gentlemen." She said.

I learned that one of the men had been in a bike accident, and the other guy had set himself on fire and jumped off a building. "This should be interesting." I thought.

The first evening in my new room was a night I will never forget. Like I said, "This should be interesting." That was an understatement.

The guy who jumped off the building on fire would not stop talking, he went on and on and on not making any sense. He would constantly walk to the doorway and call the nurse for one thing or another.

At some point he asked me a question.

"Are you the one who shot and murdered his wife?"

This was the opportunity I was waiting for.

I answered, "Yes, and I am dangerous, so you better not go to sleep tonight!"

I must have scared the heck out of him.

He started screaming for the nurse,

"Nurse, nurse get me out of here he is going to murder me!"

I wanted to scare him, but not that bad.

The officer said to him, "I won't let anything happen to you sir."

Then the officer said to me, "Don't say stuff like that."

It took hours for that guy to calm down; he didn't ask me anymore questions.

I wander if he went to sleep that night.

The next evening my mom came to visit. We were speaking for a few minutes, when the guy who set himself on fire said to my mother, "Your son said he was going to murder me."

My mom looked at me; I smiled at her like a child would smile a devious smile.

My mom said to him, "My son won't hurt you."

The next afternoon Dr. VanDyke came to speak with me, we walked to the end of the hallway where there were a few chairs.

"You said you heard a car backfire just before you shot your wife, right."

I exclaimed, "I never said that!"

"Oh, I thought you said that."

"I never said that."

He ended the conversation with, "I'll be in to see you soon."

I told my family about what he insinuated.

My brother, Johnny said, "He was trying to slip you up."

"He fooled me, I thought he was serious."

The day before I was to leave the hospital the doctors who performed the surgery came in, one explained about the damage I had done to myself.

He said, "The only thing that was left intact was your tongue, we don't know how you missed it. We pushed the teeth we could save back into place. Your upper jaw was shattered and almost all your lower jaw is missing. You're going to need several more surgeries at some point in time, were going to try to have them done at the Veterans Hospital. In the meantime, you will have to go with the police."

I said, "It's difficult for me to believe how well of a job you doctors accomplished on my face, thank you."

The next morning the 22nd of December my 29th day in the hospital I was going to embark on another new journey of my life.

Dr. VanDyke came in.

"We are going to recommend to the court that you be taken to Whiting Forensic Institute. You have a long road ahead of you, stay strong, Mr. LaPointe."

I later learned that Whiting was the maximum-security unit for the criminally insane. It was located at Connecticut Valley Hospital in Middletown.

Later that morning the police came to take me to the courthouse. Mary gave me a kiss on the cheek, I said my good-byes. The officer went to put handcuffs on me.

I asked him, "Could you wait till were downstairs before you put them on."   "Yes, I'll do that for you."

"Thank you."

BATTELL HALL
CONNECTICUT VALLEY HOSPITAL

The police transported me to the New Haven Superior Court House for my arraignment.

Outside the courtroom my mother, father and stepmother were there waiting. We waited about twenty minutes before my public defender arrived.

"I'm Anthony Demayo, I am sorry for being late, Mr. LaPointe. I am going to ask the judge to order you to be sent to Connecticut Valley Hospital for a thirty-day psychiatric evaluation."

We entered the courtroom; I sat in the rear of the room.

The judge entered and asked, "Where is the lad?"

My attorney pointed to me.

The judge looked at me for a few seconds, and then said, "I see no reason why he should not be sent to the State Hospital for evaluation."

A sheriff of the court came over to me.

"You'll have to come with me."

I said my goodbyes. I was taken downstairs to a holding cell where I sat for about a half an hour.

During that half an hour I tried to come to some kind of understanding, some kind of acceptance of the road I was about travel. I knew there would be consequences, I knew I was going to have give-up the freedom I knew, to what extent, I would have to wait and see.

Two sheriffs came over; one opened the cell.

"Mr. LaPointe were leaving to go to the hospital.

As he put the cuffs on me, I prepared myself to be put in the back of a patty wagon. They walked me through a door which opened into a large bay where the vehicles were parked. They then led me through another door, this one opened to the outside. I looked for the patty wagon, there was none. There was just one vehicle, a Mercury Marques. One of the sheriffs opened the back door and I climbed in.

As we left the courthouse the driver asked me, "Are you comfortable?" "Are the handcuffs too tight?"

I answered, "Yes" to the first question and "No" to second one.

"We will arrive at the hospital in about 45 minutes. Sit back and relax, I'll turn on the radio for you."

As we drove, I kept wandering, what was Whiting going to be like? I still, at this point, was not aware that it was a maximum-security unit for the criminally insane.

After we had driven for about 35 minutes the driver pulled into a McDonalds.

He asked, "Are you hungry?"

"I don't have any money."

"Do you like cheeseburgers and fries?" "What kind of soda do you like?"

"I thank you, but I am unable to eat solid food. I would like a cup of coffee though, just cream."

When they finished their lunch, the driver said, "We will be there in 5 minutes."

We drove onto the grounds of Connecticut Valley Hospital. We passed building upon building; some looked abandoned and very old. Others, although they were not new, looked in good conditioned.

I wasn't aware of it then, but I would be here and would walk these grounds for the next seven years.; Except for the one year I would be in the Veterans Hospital having reconstructive surgeries.

The driver turned left into a circular drive that had a few parking places to the right. He parked in front of the building which had a sign over the entrance that read Battell Hall.

I thought to myself, "Why am I here? I am supposed to go to Whiting."

In the center of the drive is a curbed circle made of grass, which in the spring thru fall is flowered.

There is a sidewalk that extended from the front all the way to the street. There are a number of small trees and shrubs along the front and sides of the building.

It is a four-story building made of red brick.

Built onto the roof is the solarium, it has its own roof and is enclosed entirely with a linked fence.

The design and shape of the building is in the form of an "H." It has two wings to each side of it.

Attached to the left wings is an extension, this is the kitchen.

Another extension attached to the right wings is part of the Occupational Therapy Dept. (OT). The rest of the OT dept. is located in the right wing on the first floor in the front of the building.

In the left wings on the first floor is the dining hall.

In the right wing at the rear of the building is the auditorium.

On both the second and third floors are individual wards, their names are numbers starting at ward #81 thru ward #86.

Wards #81 thru #83 are located on the north side. Wards #84 thru #86 are located on the south side.

Wards #81, #82, #84 and #85 are open wards; they are only locked from 9pm to 9am.

There are only two female wards. One open ward #85 and a locked ward #86

On the fourth floor are the two locked wards, one female #86 and one male #83.

The total number of the wards is six. Each story and wing have white trimmed windows across their entire length.

The two sheriffs got out of the car and opened my door. They escorted me through two sets of glass doors which opened into a large lobby.

Around the lobby are chairs, some single and some could seat two.

There are a few coffee type tables placed throughout the lobby.

The floor is made of some type of large stone squares. Each square looked as if it is made of small stones of various colors pressed together to form it, each square has a metal border around it. The borders are about a quarter inch in thickness. I could see cracks in some of the squares, most likely caused by the building settling on its foundation over the years.

In the front of the lobby on each side of the entrance way are glass windows, they are the entire length and went from the floor to the ceiling. Each window has a large planter in front of it.

To the right is a single door, this is the office of the nursing director.

In the far-right corner of the lobby is a phone booth made of wood.

To the left of the lobby is the supervisors' office. The entire front wall of it is a glass window.

There is a hallway that leads alongside the supervisors' office, it has one door on the right, and this is another phone booth.

Down the end of hall are two doors. These are the Unit Chief's offices.

At the center rear of the lobby are a set of doors that are held open leading to the elevators that are set back and to the left. Across from the elevators to the right is the laundry room. The dirty laundry is kept here until it is picked up twice a week. In between the elevators and laundry room is the rear entrance. It leads out onto a loading dock that also has a wheelchair ramp. There is also a large parking lot in the back of the building.

Also outside the lobby's rear doors are two hallways. The one to the left brought you to the canteen and dining hall.

If you took the hallway to the right, it would bring you to the medical examination room on the left.

On the right is the building supply's office and storeroom.

It then leads you through another doorway that opens into a large room usually used as a sitting area. It also has men's and woman's restrooms, and a doorway to the stair well, these are on the right.

In rear of the room on the left are a set of double doors that opened to the auditorium.

To the right at the end of the hallway is the OT dept. There are also a couple of offices and a copying room.

I stood in the lobby while one of the sheriffs went into the supervisors' office with the paperwork. When he returned, they brought me thru the open double doors, we walked down the hallway to the right to the medical examination room.

Inside, there was a doctor.

He said, "Sit on the examining table."

I sat down; one of the sheriffs took off the cuffs.

"We'll see you in thirty days."

The doctor began checking me over.

"What happened?" He asked.

I broke into tears.

"I killed my wife."

I think what he was actually asking was, what happened to my face. I don't know why I said what I said.

A few seconds later these two men dressed in suits came in. They took one look at me, I was still crying,

One of them said to the other, "We'll keep him here, the medical treatment is better here than at Whiting."

I wasn't aware of it then, but these two men, both of whom were top forensic psychiatrists, were going to play very important rolls in my future.

One is Dr. Lee, the Unit Chief of Battell Hall. The other is Dr. Volkening, one of the Senior Psychiatrists of Battell Hall.

After the exam a man came in.

"I'm Ken; I'm going to take you upstairs to ward 83."

We walked to the elevator, inside he took a key, and he put it in a lock labeled #4. I later learned that patients were not allowed to use the elevator; we had to walk the stairs.

I also never saw so many locks in my entire life. There were locks for everything, elevator, doors, windows, rooms, cabinets, you name it, and it had a lock.

When we reached the fourth floor we turned right out of the elevator, Ken unlocked the door that led into the hallway. We walked to the right to a door that had the number 83 on it. He opened the door and locked it behind him; in front of us was a long hallway. As we walked up the hall, there were doors on both sides. The first door on the left was the mop room. The first door on the right was a doctor's office. There were three more doors on the left, the first was the staff bathroom, the next two were the patient shower room and bathroom, and these two rooms were connected.

There were four more doors on the right, two were visiting rooms, and the third was the clothing supply room. At the end of the hall on the right was a door that led into the east dormitory. There are two dormitories. Each dormitory has two doors. The second door to the east dormitory was located in the TV room. The dormitories were named, east and west. They were named this because one faced the east and the other faced the west.

At the end of the hall on the right, protruding out alongside the door to the east dormitory is a small room. This is the medication room. Two sides of this room were made of glass windows reinforced with chicken wire in the glass. They began about four feet up from the floor and continued up for about four and a half feet, they spanned the length of the room. One side faced the east dormitory allowing the staff to see into the dormitory. The other side faced the hall between the med room and the west dormitory. The entrance to the medication room faced the day hall.

Directly across from the medication room was the west dormitory. It has a door to the right and another to the left.

To the left of the west dormitory was an exit to the stairwell. This is the door the patients used when they went to the dining room and when they left on their building passes.

In between the medication room and the west dormitory, the hallway opened up into what was called the day hall. In this room there were three tables capable of sitting four people at each table. There were also nine or ten chairs alongside two of the walls. On the right side of the day hall were two doors, one on each end, these doors entered into the TV room. On the left side of day hall were two rooms, one across from the center of the day hall, this is the nurse's station, all the staff stayed in that room. To the right of that was the isolation room. At the rear of the day hall were the outside windows. There are three sets of windows on this wall. The entire length of the right and left walls, floor to ceiling is made entirely of glass windows, except for the doors. The windows were framed with aluminum frames, each frame is about twelve inches square and reinforced with chicken wire.

The reason for all the walls being glass is so that every room could be visible from either the inside or outside. This gave the staff the capability of keeping an eye on everyone without having to leave the nurses station.

The TV room is also used as the smoking room; it is where 90 percent of the patients spent their day. As you walked into the room from the door closest to the medication room, immediately to the right was the second door to the east dormitory. Then on the wall to the right is a shelf, it is the entire length of the wall, on the bottom of the shelf is cabinets, above the shelf is more cabinets and at the very top, in the center of the wall is the TV, it is inset into the wall. The far wall and the wall to the far left are outside walls, there are sets of windows along the entire length of both the outside walls. In the top right window of the far wall is an exhaust fan to draw the smoke out of the room. The entire room is lined with seven rows of chairs, with an isle in the middle of the room. There are five chairs on each side of the isle. In the back of the room are three tables, with four chairs per table.

The isolation room is about a third the size of the day hall; it does not have any furniture in it. The wall facing the day hall and the wall facing the nurse's station are made of the framed glass windows. The two walls facing the outside have three sets of windows on each wall. There are two doors in which you can enter and exit; one entered the day hall, the other leads directly into the nurse's station.

These rooms today are named time out rooms or quiet rooms. As far as I am concerned its confinement, and it's usually solitary, no matter what you name them.

Each dormitory is set up to sleep fifteen people; there are three rows, with five beds in each row. Dividing the rows are lockers that are attached together and fastened to the floor. They are about six feet high. There is an isle on both ends of the dormitory. There is an outside wall on both the right and left side of the dormitory, with sets of windows the entire length of the dormitory. At the rear of the dormitory there is a fire exit that leads to a stairwell. This exit door is always locked. The doors into the dorms are kept locked. They are only opened twice a day, once for an hour after lunch and again after evening meds when everyone is allowed to go to bed for the night.

As you entered into the patient bathroom from the first doorway, straight ahead on the left are the toilet stalls. There are two urinals and four toilet stalls. If you entered in from the second door, there are five sinks to the right. There are mirrors above each sink, they are not glass mirrors; instead of glass they use stainless steel plates fastened to the wall. It is very difficult to see your reflection. The bathroom area is designed so you could walk around the entire room; it is in the shape of a rectangle.

The shower room door is directly to the left if you entered in from the second doorway. In the center of the shower room are two benches, each one about twelve feet in length. The left wall has three shower stalls. The wall across from the shower stalls was made into square cubicles to hold your clothes while you showered. Towards the back of the shower room and to the left are two tubs side by side. The entire back walls of both rooms have sets of windows, three sets in the shower room and five sets in the bathroom.

The two visiting rooms are not very large, but plenty large enough for six to eight people to visit in privacy. There are two tables and eight chairs in each of the rooms. Three walls of the room are solid walls, not framed glass like the others. The door has a window in it, which was about three by four feet in size with chicken wire in it. The back wall has two sets of windows.

The clothing supply room is not very large. When you entered the room there is shelves on both sides of a backwards L shaped isle. Against the back outside wall where there are three sets of windows. The shelves started at floor level and continue up about seven feet. They are sectioned off into square bins that are about eighteen inches wide, three feet high and eighteen inches deep. In these bins are a large variety of State issued clothing, from underwear, socks, pants, shirts, pajamas, and bathrobes. To sheets, blankets, slippers and shower sandals.

Every outside wall on the ward has steel meshed screens in every window; they could only be opened with a key. It would be nearly impossible to penetrate these screens. The mesh is made of a very fine weave of steel. The largest thing I have seen that will fit into the fine holes in the mesh is the head of a pencil.

The walls around the entire ward, and all the walls in the hallways, including the shower and bathrooms are shaped like cinder blocks, and they are about the same size. The end blocks at the corners of the walls are rounded to fit around the corners. They are a light green and they have a smooth glossy finish. The walls in the entire building are like this, except for the lobby and some of the offices.

Every floor on the entire ward has the same commercial strength linoleum; it is an ugly dark green.

This ward is designed to have a patient capacity of 30, but if there aren't 60 patients on this ward at any given time, there aren't any. The ages of the patients range from 18 to 65 years of age.

This ward is locked and heavily staffed for a reason. At any given time, a crisis could arise. The crisis could be for anyone of a number of reasons. When there are 60 people confined to two rooms, for the most part, that are designed to only hold 30, situations are inevitable, even with mentally stable people. Now you take that same number of people, some who are severally retarded and others who are so psychotic, they're not in contact with reality, and could be thinking of who knows what. Then you add those people who are so angry because they're in this environment, you have created a very volatile environment that could explode at any second.

Ken led me to the nurses' station where there were three other mental health workers, including Ken, and a nurse.

They all said, "Hello."

Then one of them said, "I'm Paul, the lead mental health worker, because this is a secure ward, and due to your situation and legal issues, you will be on constant observation. Someone will be with you twenty-four hours a day. You have to take everything out of your pockets and remove your belt. You will not be allowed to have anything other than the clothes you're wearing. Do you have any questions?"

I asked, "Will I be able to smoke?"

"Not for a while, till we see how you do."

The nurse introduced herself, "I'm Pam, the first shift nurse, I need to ask you a few questions, are you taking any medications?"

"At the hospital I was taking pain medication?"

"Do you know the name of that medication?"

"I think it was Percocet."

"I will ask the doctor on call if he will give an order for that?"

She then gave me what is called a mental status exam.

She asked me various questions, "Do you know where you are, what day of the week is it, and do you know who the president is?"

When she finished, she said, "We need you to give us some urine, can you go now?"

"Yes" I answered.

Paul said, "Ed, I will be watching you for the first hour. Come with me, I'll take you to the bathroom."

He opened a cabinet and removed a bag that contained a urine cup. He then walked me to the bathroom. He handed me the cup. I took the top off and urinated in it, put the top back on and handed it back to him.

We walked back, but we did not go into the nurse's station. Instead, we went to the door of the isolation room. He opened the door, I went in.

Paul asked, "Do you want something to read?"

"No thank you."

"I will bring you a chair."

He brought in a chair.

"Try to relax. Later today or tomorrow a doctor will come to speak with you."

The chair he brought in was made of metal; it had neither arms nor a cushion on the back of it. Other than that chair there was nothing else in the room.

Paul sat outside the isolation room in a chair. Paul is a very short man, about 5 ft, 6 inches tall. His family had worked at Connecticut Valley Hospital for three generations, there is even a street on the hospital grounds named after his family. Paul was always jesting. He took a liking to me; he always looked out for me.

I looked out the chicken wire glass panes into the day hall and smoking room. I could see the other patients, some sitting, but most of them were pacing aimlessly about the two rooms. I could see some of them smoking, I needed a cigarette bad.

It was just a few minutes later when I heard one of the staff yells, "Lunch."

The patients stormed out of the smoking room; you would think they'd have not eaten for days. They all lined up at the door that led downstairs to the cafeteria.

Paul opened the isolation room door.

"They'll bring you up a tray."

"I can't eat regular food; I need food that is pureed."

"They can do that for you."

After the patients went downstairs there was only myself, Paul and Pam the nurse left on the ward. Paul opened the door.

"Do you want to smoke a cigarette?"

"I sure do."

"Come on."

I had a pack of cigarettes with me when I came in, Paul went into the Nurse's station, I learned to call it the staff room. He brought me a cigarette from my pack. We went into the smoking room; he lit my cigarette. It tasted so good.

When I finished, I said, "Thank you, Paul."

"You're welcome."

He walked me back to the isolation room.

It was about forty-five minutes later when the patients returned from the dining room. Paul went into the staff room, a few seconds later another staff member, a black man named Jim, came in with my tray.

I said, "Thank you."

The tray was made of plastic with a top and bottom. I took the top off; the tray is sectioned off into four sections. Each section has plastic inserts that contained the individual portions of the meal. The meal came with a container of milk and a cup of coffee. It had a small cellophane package which contained a plastic fork, knife and spoon. It also had a packet of salt, pepper and two packets of sugar and a napkin.

The meal had a portion of what looked like sloppy joe without the bread, apple sauce, and chocolate pudding.

As I began to eat, I thought to myself, "I really need to learn to chew." But I knew my gums were still too tender.

After I ate Jim came in and took the empty tray.

"Did you have enough?"

"Yes, may I use the bathroom?"

"Come on."

When I got back to the isolation room, I walked over to the outside windows that faced out from the front of the building. There is a two-lane street that ran from left to right, this is Holmes Dr.

On the other side of it is a building named Woodward Hall, it houses the geriatric patients. It is a three-story red brick building. Like Battell, it is designed in the shape of an "H," but the wings on each end are not as long as the ones on Battell. It is built on a small knoll and is set back about a hundred feet from the street. It has a walkway that leads up to a set of steps to the front entrance. The entrance is covered by a pitched roof that extended out over a porch; it has a pillar on each end. The entire length of the building, including its two wings, is lined with windows along each story. The entire roof is pitched not flat.

In the rear of Woodward, I could see the top story and roof of a very old building, named Spears Hall. It was built in the eighteen hundred and has been abandoned for many, many years. It is built of brick, has six stories and the roofs shingles are made of slate.

To this day it is said that it is haunted. I can't even begin to imagine the horror those mentally insane people endured in those days. Back then there wasn't medication to alleviate their symptoms. Some say parts of that building have chains on the walls where they would chain people to restrain them and hose them with cold water to make them calm down.

I walked over to the windows that looked out to the right of Battell. Below me protruded the roof of the kitchen where the meals are prepared.

Alongside Battell is a driveway that leads from Holmes Dr. to the rear of Battell. In the rear is the parking lot.

Across from the driveway is the hospital chapel, named Yerbury Chapel. It is about as long as Battell is wide. It has quite a unique design. It is a huge "A" frame building with the roof extending from a height almost as high as Battell, to about ten feet from the ground. There are no windows on the sides, but there is a side entrance. The rear of the chapel is glass from bottom to top. The front faces Holmes Dr. It also is glass from bottom to top, with the entrance in the middle.

As you walk in the front entrance there is a hallway to the left and right. The center of the hallway is open; it is also open at each end. These three openings are isles into the main chapel. The center isle is twice as wide as the side isles.

The main chapel is very large; it has about twenty rows of pews on both sides of the center aisle.

At the rear of the main chapel is the alter area. To the left of that, there is an organ.

The entire stained glass window on the back of the chapel is made of solid pale green stained panes. Each pane is about fifteen inches wide, they are of various lengths, some as long as thirty feet. The panes extend from the floor to the top of the chapel. The front of the chapel is made the same as the back, but with the entrance built in the middle.

The ceiling is made of beautiful dark polyurethane stained wooden planks. There are a number of lights hung from the ceiling by rods, some twenty feet in length.

Located in the lower basement level are offices for the pastoral staff and the rabbi. There is an office for the receptionist; there is also another chapel where weekday morning service is held. The main chapel upstairs is for the Saturday Jewish service and Sunday Christian Services.

In the year 2000 a memorial garden was put in at the front of the chapel, also, a bell tower was erected outside. The bell tower has computer generated chimes that play a large variety of songs on

American holidays. It also tolls once on the half hour, and on the hour, it tolls each number of the hour time it is. The chimes and tolls are sent out through large speakers in the top of the bell tower. This chapels design is quite impressive.

In the back of both Battell and the chapel is Van Core Field it extends from the street that runs alongside Battell. It is about three football fields long and one and a half football field wide. A section of the field is a softball field.

The hospital holds its annual field day picnic in this field to this day.

I spent about a half an hour looking out the windows when the door opened, and two staff members brought in a bed that had wheels on the head and foot boards.

One of the staff members named John, said, "You can lie down and take a nap for an hour or so, if you'd like."

"Thank you." I asked him, "When can I get my pain medicine?"

"I'll check on that."

The bed was already made up with sheets and a spread. As I lay down on the bed, I thought, "This sure beats that chair."

A few minutes later the nurse, Pam, came in and gave me my pain meds.

"You can have these every four hours, if you need it."

I took the pill, I said, "Thank you."

As I lay there my thoughts were racing, I thought, "Where is all this going to lead. If the people over me deciding my fate don't understand that I was not in a right state of mind, that it not only was not premeditated, but that I had no thoughts or intentions of shooting my wife, I can end up in prison for twenty-five years to life. They might decide to lower the charges to involuntary man slaughter, even that could carry a sentence of twenty years. My only hope is to be found not guilty by reason of insanity. I asked myself, "What happens then?"

The staff decided to leave the bed in the room for the rest of the afternoon and night. I was very grateful for that.

At 4pm the second shift came on duty, Paul did not go home, I learned his normal shift is the second, but he, like many of the staff worked a lot of overtime.

A staff member yelled, "Meds."

It was time for the 4pm medications. The patients who received 4pm meds lined up at the med room door.

The door was divided in two, a top and bottom section. The bottom section had a six-inch-wide counter on it; it was as long as the breadth of the door. The staff member passing out the meds left the bottom of the door closed the top open.

Lead staff members who were not nurses but have taken a medication course could pass out meds, except for narcotics. All the anti-psychotic medication is dispensed in liquid form, this saved money, and they took effect faster than pill form. It is also a way for staff to give a patient more than has been prescribed, unlike pills that can be counted and kept track of. Liquid form comes in six- or eight-ounce bottles making it impossible to determine how many doses of different amounts have been dispensed.

This practice was against the rules, but commonly practiced. The staff knew just how much to give without endangering the patient.

This usually occurred during the evening med time. It is a way to sedate the patients who were agitated, and also so they would retire to the dorm early, and sleep through the night. This strategy worked very effectively.

I always wondered how come almost the entire ward is in bed fifteen minutes after med time. Except for a few and these are the higher functioning ones who didn't cause any problems. It took me awhile, but I finally caught on to this.

At 5:30pm I heard a staff member call, "Supper." The patients charged for the door; I still didn't understand what the big hurry was.

About fifteen minutes after they went to dinner I had to go to the bathroom, and it wasn't to urinate. The puree meals give me the runs. The only staff left on the ward was the evening nurse. I tapped on the window, she looked at me.

"I need to go to the bathroom."

"I can't let you out; you'll have to wait until they return from the dining room."

I was having a very difficult time holding it. Ten minutes went by, I knew I was not going to last until they returned. I tapped on the window again. She looked.

"I have to go, NOW!"

She shook her head, "No."

There was no getting around this, I defecated in my pants. I was not a happy camper.

I really couldn't blame the nurse for not letting me out. After all, it was my first day there. If it was me and I was a female and a person who has been charged with murder asked me to let them out, I would have said no too.

I learned this lesson the hard way. From now on I use the bathroom before they leave for the dining room.

Another twenty minutes went by before they returned.

When Paul came in with my dinner tray, he said, "Margaret said you need to use the bathroom."

"It's too late I went in my pants."

He put the tray on my bed.

"I'll bring you to the shower room."

Before we went into the shower room, we went into the supply room. He helped me pick out a pair of underwear, a state issued pair of pants and a shirt. He gave me a bar of soap and a small bottle of shampoo. He also gave me a knitted laundry bag to put my dirty clothes in. We went across the hall to the shower room. I got undressed and put the dirty clothes into the laundry bag.

In the shower room along the wall that separated it from the bathroom was a wooden cabinet that was open in the front, no doors. It was about ten feet long and six feet high. It had four rows of shelves across; the shelves were divided into bins. Towels were stacked into the bins. I took out two towels; I put them on the bench along with my state issued clothes.

Inside the shower stall was one water temperature control knob. There was no way to control the pressure and believe me these showers had very little pressure. The shower nozzle was built into the wall and could not be adjusted in any way. It took a while of trial and error to get the temperature where I wanted it.

Out of the shower I dried off and put on the state clothes. The pants were navy blue with an elastic waist band, the shirt was a green short sleeve, and it had a button missing.

I thought to myself, "I have only been here a few hours and I already feel institutionalized."

Back in the isolation room I sat on my bed and ate my supper. I thought it would be cold, but the meal trays were insulated. This time the meal was some type of chicken or turkey puree.

I lay on the bed to about 7:30 pm when I heard one of the staff yells, "Meds." Everyone lined up. It took about a half an hour to finish dispensing out the meds.

At about 8:30pm I heard one of the staff yells, "Snacks, supplies."

Snacks and supplies are passed out twice a day; once in the morning, at 10:30 and after evening meds. The hospital supplies, some snacks; cookies and crackers. Some of the patients have their own that their visitors bring in. All snacks are kept in a large, locked cabinet in the staff room.

The hospital also provided Tops and Buglers cigarette tobacco, Indian Chief Pipe tobacco and rolling papers with small rolling machines. The tobacco came in cellophane wrapped packages. The patients are allowed two packs a day. If you have your own cigarettes, you can get two packs twice a day.

The patients lined up outside the staff room to get their tobacco and personal supplies.

The staff set up a large table in the day hall where they put out the supplied snacks; they also brought out a coffee pot that held about 40 cups. The coffee made staying up all worthwhile.

It was John's hour to watch me. He opened the door and asked, "Would you like some snacks and coffee?"

"I'd like a cup of coffee."

"How do you like it?"

"Two sugars and milk."

At about 10 o'clock the day hall, TV room and isolation room lights were shut off. The dorm lights are shut off at 9 o'clock.

It was Paul's hour to watch me. When most of the other patients were in bed, Paul opened the door and asked, "Would you like a smoke?"

"Yes."

Inside the smoking room there were only four or five patients still up. They were watching the TV.

Paul lit me up, he said, "Why don't you sit down at the table with me?" We sat down. "You've been through a rough time of it, huh."

"Yes."

He said, "Don't worry; Dr. Lee is the best forensic psychiatrist in the State. He will help you."

"I hope so."

I finished the cigarette, and to my surprise he handed me another one.

"Thank You, Paul."

When I finished, he brought me to the bathroom and then back to the isolation room. He said, "I'll bring you a set of pajamas."

"Can I have my pain meds before I go to bed?"

"I'll have the nurse give it to you."

After I took my pain med and put on the pajamas, I climbed under the sheet and spread.

At about 11:30 the third shift lead mental health worker arrived. There were three staff on the third shift. They are all mental health workers; one is the lead worker, he is trained to give meds, other than narcotics. If a nurse is needed there, is one covering the entire building.

All but one second shift staff member and the nurse were left. The nurse gave report to third shift worker. She then left. By midnight the two other third shift staff arrived.

I could hear them talking. Bob, the lead worker was speaking to the others.

"We have a constant, which is here on court evaluation. He as a trake in his throat and half his jaw is gone. I haven't seen him yet. Let's go in and see him."

The three of them came in,

Bob said, "Mr. LaPointe, my name is Bob, and this is Dan and Ron. Say hello."

"Hello."

Bob said, "Go to sleep, we'll be here all night if you need anything."

They went back into the staff room. A few minutes later Dan came out, he sat outside the isolation room.

As I tried to fall asleep, my thoughts began racing, I had visions of the shooting, and the night in the Fireside Café with the guys from the mafia. A sudden shot of terror came over me. I thought, "I'm going to be killed." I jumped out of bed, there was nowhere to run.

Dan asked through the window, "What's the matter?"

"I'm scared."

"You're safe here. Try to sleep."

I returned to bed, and finally fell asleep.

The next thing I knew the lights came on. I could see the clock inside the staff room, it read 5:30. I sat up, my face throbbing with pain.

Don and Ron opened the door, Ron said, "You need to get up, were taking the bed out."

"I need to use the bathroom; I also need my pain medication."

"I'll be right back to take you into the bathroom, but you'll have to wait until the day nurse comes in to get the meds."

I was in a lot of pain, but I didn't argue." I didn't understand why the third shift building nurse couldn't come up and give it to me. This meant I would wait for at least an hour to an hour and a half.

At 6:45 the day nurse and staff came on duty. Before anything would happen, the staff would have report. I waited patiently, sitting in the little chair. I was thinking, "I hope I don't have to sit in this chair until after lunch."

At 7 o'clock the nurse, Pam, came in and gave me my Percocet.

She asked, "How was your night." She already knew from report, but she wanted to hear it from me.

It was ok; accept I became frightful when I tried to sleep. But it passed."

At 7:15 one of the staff yelled, "Dining room." Then again, as always, was the stampede to the door.

I thought, "I hope at least one male staff stays upstairs, I might get to have a cigarette." Two minutes after I had that thought, a tall black staff member came and opened the door.

"Do you want to smoke?"

"Yes."

Inside the smoking room, John handed me one of my cigarettes.

"I'm John."

"Hi, I'm Ted."

He lit my smoke and was quiet while I smoked. When I finished, he led me back to the isolation room.

"Breakfast will be up shortly."

When the patients returned from the dining room, Jim whom I had met yesterday brought my tray in. I took the top off. I had a nice surprise. There were scrambled eggs, which I knew I could gum. Also on the tray was hot oatmeal with two pads of butter melting on top of it. I added sugar and a little milk. There was coffee, too. When I finished, I thought, "That was the best meal I have had since my injury."

9 o'clock came and I was sitting in my chair. I noticed Dr. Lee go into the staff room. Every morning he made his rounds to every ward in the building.

Dr. Lee was a large man, about 6' 5" tall and weighed about 250 pounds. Rumor has it that during his college years he was a good boxer. It's also said that he likes his beer.

He spoke with the staff for 15 minutes. He would from time to time look through the glass at me, but never came in to speak with me. About 5 minutes after he left the ward, John and Jim brought in my bed.

John said, "Dr. Lee scolded us. He wants the bed in the room day and night for you to rest on."

"Thank you."

The rest of the morning and afternoon passed with nothing eventful. I have now spent my first 24 hours here.

At about 8:45 in the evening, a woman walked into the staff room, she spoke with the staff for a few minutes. She then opened the door to the isolation room.

She said, "Hello Mr. LaPointe, my name is Maggie, the evening Building Supervisor."

I said, "Hello."

"What does your mother look like?"

"She has blonde hair, and she is pretty for her age."

Maggie smiled and asked, "Would you like to see her?"

"Yes."

Maggie said, "Come with me."

She led me through the isolation room door into the staff office and out the other entrance way, through the day hall down the hallway to one of the visitor's rooms. She opened the door.

"You can visit for 15 minutes."

One of the staff stood outside the door where he could see me through the window that was in the door.

My mom was standing near one of the tables; I walked over to her and gave her a big hug.

"How are you, Ted?"

"I'm ok mom."

"The supervisor was very kind to allow me to see you, visiting hours end at 8pm. I explained to her how I was under the assumption that you had been taken to Whiting that I had gone there first. How I drove all the way from Naugatuck to see you."

She then said, "You should be very grateful you are not at Whiting; it is like a prison. I walked in the main door, and I had to speak through a speaker to someone. There was a large steel door that opened, and I stepped in, and the door closed after me and then in back of me another door opened into a waiting room. They told me that I was not there, they called over to here and found out you were here."

She had a cup of McDonald's coffee for me, and we talked for fifteen minutes, and the staff member said it was time for my mother to leave.

"I'll be here Christmas Day when we can spend more time together."

"Okay."

The staff member brought me back to the isolation room. I felt much better after seeing mom and I was able to get a good night's sleep.

The next day was Christmas Eve and I noticed that the patients on the ward seemed a little more agitated, a couple of small fights broke out and the staff would separate them for a while and also give them a PRN, a PRN is an extra dose of medication used to help the agitated patient calm down, it sedates them almost to the point of sleep.

There was this one patient that was so agitated that they gave him a PRN and then put him in the isolation room with me. I was not too happy with the thought of this guy in a locked room with me. He sat on the floor and began banging his head against one of the chicken glass paned windows. He banked his head so hard that the glass cracked, the staff came in and put him in a strait jacket and left him sitting on the floor.

After an hour they came in and said to him, "If you are ready to calm down and behave, we will take you out of the jacket and let you back onto the ward."

The patient answered, "I'll behave."

They took off the jacket and let him back on the ward.

A couple of hours later a man came into the isolation room, I recognized him as a maintenance man because of his tool belt. He had a windowpane in his arm, and he replaced the broken glass. A staff member stayed in the room with him while he changed the glass pane.

The rest of the evening went on uneventful, and I went to sleep soon after my pain meds and a cigarette.

The next morning, Christmas, they did not turn on the lights until 7am. They let everyone sleep a little longer.

I felt very good this Christmas morning, only because it was Christmas. I wished Jesus happy birthday.

After I had my breakfast Paul came in and said, "I am not supposed to do this, but what the hell, its Christmas." He let me out of the isolation room. "You can stay in the Day Hall or the Smoking Room, if you need to use the bathroom come and get me."

I said, "Yes, Paul, thank you."

I walked around the two rooms wishing everyone Merry Christmas, but not one of them wanted to hear it. I finally said, "It's the Lord's birthday, why is everyone so sad." No one answered me and a couple of them looked at me like I was from another planet.

After about five cigarettes Paul came in.

"The building supervisor is coming on the ward. I have to take you back to the isolation room."

"Okay, thanks for trusting me, Paul."

I hated going back in that room.

Later that morning Santa Clause came onto the ward, again Paul let me out of the room. Santa had a few gifts for everyone such as socks and best of all; rolling tobacco, I say this because I had finished my cigarettes. There was also coffee for us; I stayed out of the room for a couple of hours.

That afternoon my dad and stepmother came to visit. They brought me coffee, cigarettes and some clothes.

They asked how I was doing, my father said, "I got lost coming here or we would have been here earlier."

They were not able to stay very long, they had other people to visit.

My father over the years came once a week to see me, but never stayed more than an hour. I believe the place really bothered him.

Later Christmas evening my mother came to see me. My sister Cindy was with her. We talked about what I was doing and how they were treating me. I told them everyone was good to me.

I asked my mom, "How are Michael and Rene?"

"They are fine; I'm making arrangements to see them."

My mom always tried to keep my spirit up during this entire ordeal.

I have now been without any medication for some time now and the effects of being without them were beginning to take its toll on me. I was pacing back and forth in the visiting room and began crying.

"Mom, I am a proud man, I can't take being locked up. If they send me to prison, I will take my life. Mom, it was an accident, I loved Patty."

"Ted, I think you would feel calmer with some medication to help with the anxiety and the bad thoughts."

"If they give me something I will take it.

My mom went out and spoke with Paul; he said he would speak with the on call to get an order. It may take about an hour.

After my mom left, a staff member, Ted, asked me, "Do you know how to play ping pong?"

"Yes, I do." I answered.

"Let's go play a few games."

We walked out of the ward to the center hallway where the game room, called 89, was and we began playing. He was a very good player, and each game was a hard-fought battle by both of us. But the best part about it was that it took my mind off my situation.

Some time went by when Paul came in with a med cup in his hand. As he handed me the cup he said, "I was wondering how long you were going to suffer with all that is going on. This will help you relax."

After I took the meds, I ran to the other side of the ping pong table to shake hands with Ted. I startled him, my sudden move made him think I was attacking him, when I reached out my hand to him, I could see the relief on his face. I really scared him for a second. I said, "Thank you."

"You're welcome, get a good night's rest." He answered.

The medication took effect fast and the first things I realized was how my thoughts slowed down and the paranoia diminished. Within 45 minutes I was asleep.

The next couple of days went by as usual and I was allowed out of the isolation room more often and for longer periods of time.

One afternoon a severely retarded young man, who always sat on the floor outside the staff room, not because he wanted to, but because he was made to, for reasons I didn't understand until this one afternoon. He suddenly began screaming at the top of his lungs and started punching himself in the face and skull.

Three staff members came out of the staff room and two grabbed him by each arm and the other opened the isolation room and said, "Go into the smoking room until he calms down." I did as he asked.

After they put him in the room I came out into the Day Hall and watched this young man take off all his clothes and then defecated on him and the floor. He then began taking the fesses and throwing it all over the room, on the windowed walls and all over the ceiling. The staff waited until he was finished, and he had calmed down. About an hour later they let him out of the room, he went back to sitting by the staff room.

The staff went into the isolation room and wiped down the walls and mopped the floor.

A short while later it was time for the evening meal. I was asked to go back into the isolation room. The smell in that room was the worst fesses smell I think I have ever smelled. The smell stayed prevalent because they did not clean the ceiling. I had to eat my meal and spend the night smelling this.

The next morning Dr. Lee made his rounds, and he came into the isolation room and immediately walked out and began speaking with the staff.

Within 15 minutes the staff member, John, came in with a mop bucket and mop. He said, "I am sorry you had to smell this. Dr. Lee said that if he was you, he would refuse to stay in this room."

John took the mop and reached up with it and cleaned the ceiling. He opened the windows and staff door to air out the room.

The next day at lunch time, John was working, and he came to me and asked, "How would you like a job to do during the lunch break?"

I answered, "I would like that. What would you like me to do?"

"Go into the smoking room and move all the chairs and tables to one side and sweep the floor. Then you can stay in there and smoke until lunch comes up. You can do this every day from now on, if you want."

"I would like to do that, John. Thank You."

John went into the staff room and began speaking to the ward nurse. The same nurse that would not let me out of the room the day I went to bathroom in my pants. I could hear them talking. John told her what he wanted me to do, and she answered, "No, I will not stay on this ward alone with Mr. LaPointe unless he is locked in the isolation room."

John stated, "If you have read Mr. LaPointe's progress notes you would see he has not been a problem since he came on this unit."

She answered, "He cannot come out unless there is a male staff on the ward with me."

John came back to me, before he could speak, I said, "I heard her, John. I'll be okay and come out when there is a male on the ward."

John said, "I am going to see what I can do to take you off constant observation and allow you to go down to the dining room and sleep in the dorm."

"I'd like that, John."

"I'll get back to you as soon as I can get this done. In the meantime, you can come out when there is a male on the ward."

A few days later I was in the Day Hall when Dr. Lee came on the ward. He was sitting in the staff room speaking with Paul. He kept staring at me with a look that scared the heck out of me. I began walking around in circles, from time to time I'd stop and look at him, and he was still giving me that look. I believe he was determining if I was paranoid. I was, and he knew it.

When I was allowed out of the isolation room, they would leave the room open. One morning when I was sent back to the isolation room there was a naked patient in my bed. Graig, the staff member who sent me back to the room, went in and began hitting the man on the head and told him to get out of the bed, put on his pants and go into the other room.

I said, "Graig, you didn't have to hit him like that."

Graig just looked at me on his way out of the room. He slammed the door and locked it.

One morning when Dr. Lee was on the ward and speaking with the staff for a while, he had me come into the staff room.

Dr. Lee said to me, "Ted, if you promise not to try to run away or hurt yourself, I'll allow you to eat in the dining room. Also, you can sleep in the dormitory."

"I promise, Dr. Lee. Thank you for trusting me."

I had spent a total of two weeks in the isolation room and on constant observation. My observation had been lowered to constant with visible checks every 15 minutes.

That noon I went down with the rest of the ward to the dining hall. All the patients had to line up and walk through the food line where they slid their trays along the line and the dishes with the food were given to them.

The patients who had diet trays would get in a separate line and the staff would pass out their diet trays. As I was waiting for my tray a chair flew by me. Two staff ran by guess who threw the chair. If you can't guess, it was the retarded man. After the staff put him in a jacket and escorted him back to the ward a staff member said to me.

"Don't be nervous, this goes on all the time, you'll be okay."

I thought to myself, "Oh great!"

I didn't touch the meal for two reasons; one, that chair scared the heck out of me it missed me by inches. And two, I was sick and tired of the puree food they gave me.

I put the tray in the window where they did the washing of the dishes and walked over to the exit door, which was locked of course. I stood against the wall and looked over the entire dining hall.

There were two large eating areas, one to the right and one to the left. Way to the rear on the right was an area for the staff to eat. The staff on the open wards were the only ones who ate during the meals. The locked ward staff had to monitor the patients more closely.

Sitting on the floor next to me was a patient, Dominick, he looked up at me and said, "Why don't you sit down and be one of the gangs."

I sat down and realized it was not normal to sit on a floor, but on the other hand it was more comfortable than standing waiting up to 30 or 40 minutes to go back to the ward. I didn't know it then, but I would be spending many hours sitting and laying on the floors of Battell Hall.

Now that I no longer had to go into the isolation room I could smoke and watch TV as much as I wanted to. But as far as sleeping in the dormitory I had some strong fears about sleeping in a room with all these people who were not exactly in their right state of minds. Then again, how many were thinking the same thing about me?

At eight o'clock that evening medication was passed out and within a half hour there were only a few of us still awake. I stayed up until the lights were turned off, hoping by the time I went into the dormitory everyone would be asleep.

In bed a laid there awake for a long time, the tears came as I wondered how I was going make it through what was to come. I look back now, and I wish I knew there was someone with me, right there next to me that I could have talked to, a savior who knew exactly what I was going through, who knew the beginning from the end. He knew that through all this he had plans for me to someday bring glory to him. I can look back now and can say, "All things do work for good to those who love God." No matter what you are going through or have been through He is right there with you; waiting for you to cast your cares, your troubles, whatever it is on Him for He cares for you. He will never leave you or forsake you.

One afternoon as I was sitting in the Day Hall, a man came over and sat at the table with me.

He stated, "My name is Dan, what's yours?"

"I'm Ted."

"Why are you here?" He asked.

"I'm here on court charges and for a psychological evaluation."

"What are your charges?"

"I paused, and answered, "I'm charged with the shooting death of my wife and attempted suicide."

He looked at me and asked, "Was that the shooting in New Haven?"

"Yes."

He said, "I was supposed to clean that house after the shooting, but I had a relapse of my illness and came here."

That evening Dan and I were walking down the staircase to the dining room when he put out his hand and showed me some kind of powder in his palm. He said, "This is poison, I going to put it in the coffee urn."

He scared the s*** out of me! Needless to say, I didn't have any coffee that meal.

Late that evening after most everyone else had gone to bed a staff member, also named John, and a couple of us patients were watching a movie on TV. At one point in the movie there was a woman sitting in a car, she was looking out the front windshield when a man stepped in front of the car with a shotgun. He pointed the gun at the car and shot her in the face thru the window. I jumped out of my chair! I didn't know what to do or where to go. It scared me near to death! John turned to me and said, "Flash back, huh." I was messed up for days after that.

My thirty-day evaluation was almost up. Dr. Lee came to speak with me. He said, "I'm going to testify that you are competent to stand trial. You're going to have to go to jail overnight to become a penal transfer. Try not to be too nervous, you'll be back the next day."

Two days later at 9 o'clock in the morning the same two sheriffs arrived to take me to the courthouse. Again, we went in their private car, and I was handcuffed.

At the courthouse I was put in a holding cell where I stayed for about an hour before I was taken upstairs to the courtroom.

In the courtroom there was only the prosecutor, my attorney, Dr. Lee and the Judge.

Dr. Lee was put on the stand, he testified to the court, "Mr. LaPointe was totally out of contact with reality the night of the shooting. He needs to be hospitalized, to be stabilized on medication. It's my opinion that Mr. LaPointe is competent to stand trial." The Judge replied, "I find the defendant competent to stand trial. He is to be taken to the county jail for penal transfer, where he is then to be transferred back to Connecticut Valley Hospital to await his Grand Jury hearing."

My attorney said to me, "At the jail you will be put in the hospital section, you will be sent back to the hospital tomorrow morning.'

I was brought downstairs to the holding cell where I waited over two hours to be taken, by patty wagon, to the county jail.

When I arrived at the jail, I was put in a holding cage, I say cage because it was a room encased by meshed fenced wire. The cage had metal benches to sit on. There were three other prisoners in the cage with me.

I waited over two hours to be processed. This consisted of having fingerprints and mug shot taken.

I was then taken to a room where they had me empty my pockets and take off my clothes. They searched me thoroughly but did not see my matches and cigarettes. God is good. I can say this looking back; that he had them miss the cigarettes and matches.

I was then taken to the hospital block of the jail. There was a long corridor with an examination room on the side. Further down on the right was the guard station. I was taken to my cell where the guard said, "You will be having a medical examination in a short while." He locked the cell.

The cell was about 12 by10 and had a small sink, a toilet made of stainless steel, and the bed was a metal cot with a mattress three inches thick. There was only on sheet to cover myself with and. it was very uncomfortable to lie on. The cell was cold and damp.

Right then I made a vow to myself and God: If I go to prison, I will take my life!

A couple of hours later the guard came and took me to the examination room where the doctor gave me a quick exam. I was then taken to the guard station where the guard said, "If you don't want any problems while you're here: don't give us any trouble."

I said, "I won't cause any problems."

The phone rang, the guard answered it and said to the person on the other end: "He is standing right here." The guard handed me the phone, it was Dr. Lee, he said; "Don't be nervous, we'll have you out of their first thing in the morning."

I replied, "I'll be okay."

As I was being brought back to the cell the guard said, "You'll be eating dinner in about an hour."

I waited until he was down the end of the hall and then lit a cigarette. I sat there thinking; "I would rather be in the isolation room than sitting in this cell."

There was a prisoner in the cell across from me who was yelling and banging on the cell door, demanding a cigarette. He continued this until the guard came and let him out of the cell to have dinner.

I was taken to a small room where there were a few chairs and a couple of small tables. There were three other inmates in the room with me.

The guard brought in the dinner trays. The meal consisted of chicken, potatoes, and corn. There was a container of milk and a strong cup of coffee, which was what I needed. I couldn't eat the meal because it wasn't ground up. I gave my meal to the guy who was yelling in his cell. I felt sorry for the guy. In return he gave me his coffee.

About a half hour later we were brought back to our cells.

Back in my cell I smoked a couple of cigarettes with the coffee. About 8 o'clock they brought me my medication and a short while later the lights were turned off.

As I laid there, I asked the Lord to help me go to sleep. The next thing I knew it was morning. The Lord really does hear us.

They brought me breakfast, which consisted of hot cereal, that wasn't hot. There was also toast, milk and coffee.

I laid back down when I heard the guard say, "You'll be leaving soon."

But soon wasn't soon enough for me.

A few minutes later he came back and unlocked the door. He said, "When you're dressed come to the guard station."

I still had almost a full pack of cigarettes and plenty of matches. So, I walked across to the cell where the man that wanted to smoke was. I made sure the guards were not looking and gave him the smokes and matches. He didn't say anything, but I could see he was very grateful. I bet that guy didn't yell anymore for quite a while.

I didn't know it then but these many years later I learned that God blesses us to be a blessing. I think I did a good thing that day.

They brought me out to where the holding cage was, there the sheriff not only put handcuffs on me but angle shackles also.

We went to the garage where I was put in the back of a state car. There was a cage between the back and front seats. I was soon on my way back to Battell Hall.

When we arrived, we did not go directly to Battell Hall, we stopped at the administration building, Shew Hall. The sheriff took me inside where we went into an elevator, two women also got in with us. I thought to myself, "These two women must think they are in an elevator with a mad man." At the fourth floor we went to the Superintendent's Office. Inside his office he signed the transfer papers and said to the sheriffs, "Take him over to Battell."

At Battell, they took me into the lobby, I saw a nurse from my ward walking through; when she saw me, she smiled, as if to say, "It's good to have you back."

The supervisor said to the sheriff, "You can take the hardware off of him here." They took of the cuffs and shackles and left.

A staff member took me to the ward. I actually felt grateful to be back.

That afternoon I called my mom, I told her all about my trip to the jail. I asked, "When do you think you'll be up to see me?"

She replied, "I'll be up tonight about 6 PM. I'll see you then."

I went into the TV room, while I was smoking one of the patients, Mike, asked, "Do you have a quarter for a cup of coffee?" I handed him a quarter, he took it and exclaimed, "Why did you give this to me?!" He gave it back, only to ask me for it again a minute later. I gave it to him again. This time he drew back his arm as far as he could get it and let me have it right in my trake. He expected me to drop, but I stood up and said, "What the hell is wrong with you!" But no words came out, when he hit my trake the Q tip came out, so no verbal sound came out. He took off like a scared rabbit. He hadn't expected me to take the punch.

I went to Paul and told him what had happen.

Paul asked, "Are you okay?"

"It's sore, but I'm okay."

Paul insisted I see the doctor.

Mike was put into the isolation room for a few hours.

While I was waiting in the TV room another staff member came in and asked me, "What happened?"

I answered, "Mike asked me for a quarter and when I gave it to him, he yelled, why did you give this to me?! And then he punched me in the throat."

He said, "I don't believe that is all that happened."

Then one of the other patients spoke up and said, "That is what happened, I was standing right there, Mike hit him for no reason."

The staff member left the room.

A little while later the doctor came on the ward and looked at my trake and said what I already knew, "There's no damage."

When Mike was finally let out of the isolation room, he came to me and said, "Ted, I'm sorry."

I answered, "that's okay, Mike, I just don't understand why you did it."

He didn't have an answer, he just walked away.

Mike was a very troubled, angry young man; he would lose his temper in a second for no apparent reason. A number of years later I learned he had died. It was said that he either jumped or got pushed out of a 19-story building in New York City. I believe it could very well have been either one of those two.

I didn't mention this, but I had now been taking medication since the night Paul first gave it to me and now only taking the pain medication, usually once or twice a day, mostly when I first wake up in the morning, that is when I seem to have the most pain.

The psychotropic medication was Melarill, for the most part it relieved the paranoia, but it had a couple of serious side effects. They are sensitivity to the sun and some sexual side effects. The latter, I, at that time, was not concerned about.

My father came to visit me one afternoon. While we sat in the visiting room drinking the coffee he brought, he said, "The VA hospital has refused to admit you to perform the surgery you need. I contacted the State Representative and explained your case and that you were a Viet Nam era Marine veteran. The Representative said he would contact the VA hospital and get back to me."

The following week Dr. Lee came on the ward to speak with me, he said, "Tomorrow we are going to transport you to the VA for a surgical evaluation. While you are there you will be under the care and supervision of the VA. You should be back in a couple of days. Is this okay with you?"

I answered, "Yes, I'll do okay there, Dr. Lee."

"See you when you get back."

Two day later, first thing in the morning, I was transported to the VA hospital in West Haven.

When we arrived the staff member who transported me brought me to the surgical ward on the 4th floor, west wing. I was left with a nurse and the staff member left.

I then went through the routine of having my vital signs taken, blood and urine samples given. I was then brought to my room.

Soon after I was in my room a male steward came in and said, "I am to be with you at all times, if you need to use the bathroom or need something just ask me."

That evening a woman came in, I don't recall her name, but she was a plastic surgeon and she sat and talked with me for over an hour. I explained what had happened; she listened and then looked at my injury. She then said, "We can do a bone graft with some bone and muscle from one of your ribs or some other area. Your jaw will be wired shut for six to eight weeks. As far as your bottom lip there is not much we can do except make your mouth a little larger so it will open further. You will always have some scaring, but the surgeons at Yale did a nice job. Do you have any questions for me?

"No, you explained everything, but do you know when the surgery will take place?"

"Scheduling will have to be determined; you will be contacted. Tomorrow we'll take some x-rays and the next day you can return to CVH."

"Thank you, Doctor."

Not long after she left the room the Head Nurse came in and spoke with the steward who was watching me. The steward then left the room and the nurse said to me, "The Dr. you spoke with said you are to be left on your own to go where you please, just let the desk know where you are going. You can go outside to smoke and there is a canteen downstairs."

I couldn't believe what she just told me. I can look back now and can see it was the favor of God on my life. Time and time again things like this happened to me, even when I went astray and messed up, which was many, many times over the following 30 or more years. He is faithful and if he has called you, you can't get away; He'll just keep drawing you back. That is unless you totally hardened your heart. All things do work for good to those who love God and are called according to His purpose.

I figured I had a day or so to enjoy this freedom and I was going to take advantage of it. I went down to the cafeteria bought a cup of coffee and went out to smoke. I still couldn't believe I was walking around by myself. I thought to myself, "I could, if I wanted to, take off and run, but that isn't who I am. I will see this through to the end."

The next day I had all the x-rays and just hung out. The following day I would be on way back to CVH.

The morning I was to return to CVH. At around noon time I was sitting on my bed, when Mickey, who was my best friend before all this happened, walked into my room. He looked at me, put a big smile on his face and just shook his head. I gave him a big hug and he asked, "How are you holding out?"

"Like you, Mick, I am an ex-jar head, we don't surrender." For those who don't know what a jar head is, it is a Marine.

As we were speaking the nurse came in and said, "Your ride is on the way to pick you up. You can wait here or down at the front entrance."

Mickey came with me to the front entrance, and we sat on a bench while I waited for my ride to arrive.

Mickey turned to me and asked, "Do you want a joint?"

"I don't think I can handle that just yet, but thanks."

We talked for about a half an hour when I saw the State car drive up.

I said to Mick, "Take it easy."

He answered, "You're the one who needs to take it easy."

I went and got into the car.

A few days after returning to CVH Dr. Lee came to see me again. This time he had some news I didn't want to hear. He said, "The director of the VA Hospital called me and said, they won't admit you to the hospital to perform the surgery until your charges are finalized. If you are not acquitted, they will not do the surgery. It may be a couple of years before you go to trial. I know you want the trake taken out, but you will need it for the surgery, so I suggest you let it stay in until then. I know it is a little uncomfortable, can you put up with it?"

"I can deal with it."

One morning I was sitting in the smoking room when a woman came into the smoking room. She walked up to me and said, "Hello Mr. LaPointe, I'm Dr. Johnson, I'm going to be your treating psychiatrist. I would like to speak with you for an hour or so, can you come with me?"

We went into one of the visiting rooms where she said, "I need to document for your medical chart exactly what occurred leading up to and the shooting. Do you feel up to that?"

"I guess so," I replied.

I then told her the entire story, the memory brought back the sorrow and fears. When I finished, I had tears in my eyes. What I didn't expect was that she had tears in her eyes too.

She asked, "Are you alright to go back onto the ward?"

"Yes, Dr. Johnson."

"I'll check on you once a week to see how you are doing."

There was a young man on the ward with me named Jim, both I and my father took a liking to him. When my father came to visit, Jim always wanted to sit and talk with us. I believe he respected my father because his father was in and out of prison and Jim kept heading in that direction. He also, was in the hospital for evaluation, after being arrested for breaking and entering.

My dad had a personality that drew people to him; he was friendly and always had encouraging words for people. He grew up during the depression and went into the Army Air Core, today it's the Air Force. He was a Tech Sgt. and flight engineer and top turret gunner in a B-17 during World War II. On his 21st birthday and what was to be his final combat mission, his plane was shot down over enemy territory.

After helping one of the waist gunners who had been wounded in the groin area put on his chute and bail out. My dad went to another gunner who was lying on the deck and in sheer terror whose chute had opened inside the plane. My dad checked the guidelines on the chute; they were in tack and not twisted. My dad rolled up the chute and put it in the gunner's arms and told him to bail out. The gunner would not go, by that time another flack explosion hit the plane and blew my father out of the plane.

As he parachuted to the ground a German spotter plane flew by him, as he flew by my dad saw the pilot give him a salute. As soon as he was on the ground two German solders dressed in uniforms that had the image of a skeleton on them came and captured him. He was taken to Star lock 17, a prisoner of war camp, where he spent 19 months, until he was liberated by Patton's Army.

One day Jim came and asked, "Ted, could I wear one of your jeans to go on my building pass, I don't want to go wearing State clothes."

"Sure, you can, Jim."

Well, it turned out he took more than a building pass. He walked across the field to Dutcher Hall, the drug and alcohol unit, to see some of his old friends.

Security brought him back.

That was the end of his building passes for a while.

I asked him, "How did you get all wet?"

He took me to the window and said, "Look, see my tracks?"

I couldn't help but see them they were the only tracks in the whole field. He walked through 10 inches of snow to see his friends. I looked at him and we both laughed.

February came around and I was determined to get off that soft diet. I asked Dr. Johnson, "Can you let me try eating a regular diet?"

"Of course, you can, if you feel you're able to eat it. They won't give it to you until I put in the order, so you can start at breakfast."

At breakfast I went through the chow line for the first time. The breakfast consisted of hard-boiled eggs, although I did eat these before a couple of times. Also, there was toast and hot cereal. This was an easy meal to eat, and the toast was the only thing new to me.

I learned how to eat all the food they served. Sometimes it took a while to gum the meats into small soft pieces, but it was all worth the work, just to taste whole food.

I had now been on unit 83 for two months and I felt I was ready to be transferred to one of the open wards. I waited for Dr. Johnson to come on the ward.

I stopped her and asked, "Dr. Johnson can I be transferred to an open ward?"

She answered, "No."

"I'm not going to hurt anyone or myself, I promise."

"Ted, I can't allow that at this time." She walked away.

I was very disappointed; I thought she would allow me.

One evening, Ted, not the other Ted I spoke of, but the second shift lead mental health worker, who had an artificial leg, was working. As he was letting the patients with building passes off the ward, I noticed he was letting certain patients who did not have building passes of the ward. So, I figured I had nothing to lose, so I asked him, "Ted, can I go to the canteen for a soda?"

He replied, "Because of the seriousness of your charges I shouldn't let you go."

"Ted, I promise, I won't run."

He said, "Okay, a half an hour. Don't make me come looking for you."

"Thanks Ted."

I went down the stairwell to the ground floor. When I reached the door to the dining room, I then realized I had no idea where to go. There was another stairwell, but that went down to a locked door, a dead end. I went back up to the dining room door, there was only one other door, that lead to the outside, I figured that would be locked for sure. I went and tried to open it and sure enough it opened. I walked to the left to the front entrance and went in. I could hear music coming from near the elevators, I followed the music, and it was from a juke box in the canteen.

Inside the canteen I saw the juke box against the back wall. There were two rows of tables; one row along the wall to the left and the other row along the right wall where there were windows all the way down to the canteen counter.

The canteen counter was L shaped with a small counter to the far right where the various candy bars were kept. It had a glass front. On the wall directly in back of the cash register were cigars and tobacco on shelves. Against the left wall behind the counter was a refrigerator. Against the back wall was a small desk and to the far-right wall was a freezer. Next to the cash register was a soda fountain. This is how the service area is set up.

Dan, from my ward was working; the canteen was run by patients who were on a work program.

I asked Dan, "Could I get a cup of coke?"

He asked, "How did you manage this?" As he was pouring my soda.

I answered, "Ted let me down, but I have to go right back. I'll see you upstairs."

I felt uncomfortable, so I decided to go back up to the ward. At the ward door I knocked, and Ted let me in.

I said, "Thanks Ted."

He answered, "I knew I could trust you."

Also on the ward with me was a young man, name Louie. He was not only from my hometown, but was, at one time, very close friends with my brother Keith.

Louie kept to himself and said very little to anyone. He was very short and when he walked, he would lean way over to one side. It hurt me to see him so ill.

He would always ask to come into the visiting room when my dad would come to visit me. My dad made him feel welcome and right at home, even though Louie would just pace around the room. Also, my dad always brought him a cup of coffee. When he finished the coffee, he would just walk out without saying anything, but I know he was grateful.

One evening my brother, Keith, came to visit. We talked for close to an hour when he said, "I'm going to leave. Do you want a joint?"

I answered, "How am I going to smoke it here?" I thought for a moment and said, "Okay."

He gave it to me and left.

Carrying that joint around made me very nervous and I tried to think of how I was going to smoke it with no matches and besides, someone was bound to smell it.

That evening there was a staff member who I knew got high, don't ask me how I knew but one addict can always spot another addict.

When it was time to go to the game room, I waited until he was alone and I walked up to him and asked, "Do you want to smoke a joint?" I was scared, very scared.

He looked at me like I was out of my mind asking him that question. He answered, "Stay right here, I'll be right back.

All I could think was, "He is going to get back up to bring me into the isolation room. But, to my surprise he came back alone.

He had a coat on and another patient coat in his hand. He said, "Let's go outside."

We went down the elevator and out the loading dock door. We walked to the back of the parking lot, to the edge of the field where there was a picnic table.

I took out the joint and we talked as smoked it. When it was finished, I thought we were going to leave, but he pulled out another one. I got very high to say the least and also was having some intense paranoid thoughts.

We went back upstairs, just before we went on the ward, he asked, "What are you going to do about your eyes?"

I answered, "Don't worry; I'm going straight to bed. Good night and thanks."

In bed I had to fight the thoughts of fear coming over me. I realized then that smoking pot did not help matters at all. But the truth is, over the next seven years I continued every chance I had. I still don't know why I tortured myself like that.

The reason I mentioned this, and other times I got high; mentioned throughout this book is to show how I was so soon removed from that prayer I prayed in intensive care; to be like Jesus. I still believed in Him, but where I failed was, I didn't seek to get to know him. I didn't have teachers, and honestly; I didn't know the bible, I didn't know it teaches how to conduct our lives. I can honestly say that I didn't know what the bible had in it.

The drug and alcohol abuse continued until 1989, when I got caught by having a positive urine during my second stay at CVH. That was the major turning point in my life.

One morning I was smoking a cigarette when Sweets, a blind black man, but I must tell you, I am not sure he is blind, at least not totally. He always knew if you were smoking. He would walk up beside you and put his hand in your face. This was his way of asking for a cigarette.

He came over and put his hand in my face, I pushed it away, and he put it back in my face. This went on for three or four times when I finally pushed his hand and him to the side. He then let me have it right in the chest; the blow broke my chain which had a cross on it that I wore around my neck. He walked away like nothing happened. I asked God in my thoughts, did this break because I didn't give him a smoke?" Of course, I know today that wasn't the case at all. The truth is, I hated not giving out cigarettes, but I could go through a pack in fifteen minutes if I gave one to everybody who wanted one. I wish I was able to do that.

There were two deaf and dumb men of our ward, Sammy and Johnny. Sammy would just walk around the ward looking for someone doing something wrong. When he spotted something, he would begin to make a loud noise, which I can't describe on paper, and point at the person. He would continue this until he got someone's attention or the person, he was pointing at stopped whatever he was doing.

Sammy had been on so much Thorazine for so long that his face was a very bright red color. If you saw him for the first time you might think he wasn't breathing, that is how red his face was.

Now Johnny was a quiet man and he had himself a little hobby; He would take a piece of paper and a sharpened pencil and go to one of the mesh screens on a window and put the paper up against the screen. He then took the pencil and began to punch holes into the paper. The holes were not random, but as you watched he would spell out his name in the paper. The spelled-out letters were the same length and in perfect alignment. It was interesting to watch him do this.

I was now on the locked ward for three months and it has now been about a month since I had asked Dr. Johnson if I could go to an open ward.

One afternoon I was sitting in the smoking room, Paul came up to me and said, "Ted, get your things together, you're going down to ward 82", which is one of the male open wards.

I couldn't believe my ears. I asked, "Are you kidding me?" I jumped up, went into the dorm, threw my clothes into a bag and went to the staff room with a huge smile on my face. The staff were as happy about it as I was. I don't know if that was good or bad.

Paul said, "You've worked hard and have earned this, Ted. We'll be seeing you. Enjoy your new freedom."

Ward 82

Ward 82 was directly below Ward 83. it was one of four open wards. The Charge Staff member on the ward was a woman named Mrs. Norton. Her husband was the Fire Chief of the CVH Fire Department, yes, the hospital had its own fire department and its own police department.

Both Mr. and Mrs. Norton had a reputation of ruling with an iron fist. I learned quickly that that was an understatement.

When I walked unto the ward, I was totally astounded by what I saw. Compared to Ward 83 it was a castle, cleaned to the point of being spic and span.

It was set up much the same way as Ward 83 except the smoking room was not combined as a TV room. It was smaller with a couple of tables and chairs along the outside wall. There was also a radio to listen to.

The Day Hall had comfortable cushioned chairs with various plants throughout the room.

The TV room was to the left of the Day Hall and was very large. It was the same size as the entire Day Hall. There were a couple of couches and chairs and plants throughout the room. The TV was on a counter and there were bookshelves along the same wall as the counter.

I was only on the ward a few minutes when I met Mrs. Norton. We sat down and she proceeded to inform me about the ward rules and schedule for the ward.

She said, "You'll be free to come and go off the ward between the hours of 9am and 9pm. You have to be here on time for your medications. I see you only receive medications in the morning and evening, which will be 8am and 9pm.

You will be allowed to stay up as late as you like, but you have to be out of bed at 7am.

You can smoke whenever you like, and you can carry your own lighter or matches. The smoking room is open all night if you want to get up during the night and smoke.

The lights are turned on a 7am and ward chores begin at 7:30 am and are to be finished after breakfast. You will be assigned a new chore every two weeks.

The dormitories are locked after breakfast and are only opened for one hour after lunch. You can get whatever you need from your locker at this time. They are opened in the evening at 8pm.

All the open wards eat meals at the same time. If you are out on your pass, you do not need to come to the ward before meals. You can go to the dining hall during the one hour that it is opened for lunch and dinner.

Dr. Johnson has issued you a building pass, it allows you to go anywhere in the building, it includes the immediate outside area of Battell. "Do you have any questions?"

"No, Mrs. Norton."

She said, "Well if you think of any don't be afraid to ask."

I put my coat on and went downstairs to the canteen for a cup of coffee. As I sat at a table I had a new outlook on things, it is funny how just the privilege of being able to walk around a building can remind someone of how precious freedom is.

It came time for lunch, and I went into the dining hall. There is a set menu for the meals, and they rotated them for a month and then a new menu would start. The only menu that is constant was the breakfast menu.

As I sat eating my lunch, I began listening to the conversations between other patients sitting around me. The conversations seemed not to make any sense to me but, they seemed to know exactly what they were saying to each other.

After I finished my meal, I went into the lobby and sat in one of the chairs. It wasn't more than five minutes when one of the day supervisors came out and said, "Patients are not allowed to sit in the lobby, it's for visitors."

Both of the day supervisors had the same first name, Donna. They were known as the deadly D's. They had little to no compassion for the patients.

I went into the hallway just outside the lobby where there was a man sitting on the floor. I asked, "Can I sit with you?"

"Sure, you can," He answered.

I sat down and he said, "My name is Norm. What is yours?"

"Hi Norm. I'm Ted."

We sat and talked until 1pm when the canteen opened.

Norm was also on the same ward as me and we became very close friends. We would talk about why we were in the hospital, Norm, like me was arrested for a crime. He was arrested for sexual assault, found guilty and sentenced to 5 years in jail. He was in jail for less than a week when he cut his wrists in a suicide attempt. They transferred him to CVH for evaluation. After speaking with Dr. Lee and explaining what had actually occurred, he was allowed to finish his time at CVH.

Norm explained to me what had occurred with the girl he was accused of raping. He explained how he was out riding his motorcycle and had stopped for fuel. A young woman came up to him and they began speaking. She asked if he would take her for a ride and he said he would. As they were riding, she began rubbing his chest and then between his legs. They rode to a back road where they had sex. He said it was consensual and he hadn't forced her in any way. He rode her back to the gas station and a few days later he was arrested.

Norm's wife of many years filed for divorce, and he lost his contact with his children.

I would, from time to time, walk up to Norm in the hallway where we sat, and he would be crying. He truly regretted what he had done and like me it cost dearly.

There was another man on my ward that I had become very close friends with. His name was Ralph. Unlike Norm and me he at that time was a volunteer patient. But Ralph also had an arrest back about 14 years earlier when he was charged with the second-degree manslaughter of his nephew. Although Ralph was not in his right state of mind when the crime was committed and had a long history of mental illness he was told while in jail by a forensic psychiatrist, "I want you to know I don't believe in the insanity law, so if that is your defense, I am against it."

Ralph was found guilty and sentenced to 15 years. He was paroled after 7 years and immediately signed himself into a psychiatric hospital.

Ralph has an aunt who stuck by him the entire time since his arrest and came to visit him every week. She was the only relative that had known he was not a murderer.

While in prison Ralph's parents were killed in a plane crash that went down in the ocean. His father was the last soul to be found.

Ralph's parents had taken out an insurance policy the day of the plane crash which went to Ralph and his brother. Ralph when he was released from prison spent the money on psychiatric hospitals and therapy. Which led to little or no relief, he stated he had better care in the State Hospital.

I was on the open ward for about a month and made the decision to call Linda, the woman I was in the bar with the night of almost being shot. I had thought long and hard about whether or not I should contact her. I wanted her to know she had nothing to do with what had happened and to say our good-byes.

I found her number in the phone book and called. We spoke for a while and she said she wanted to come visit me but, had no idea how to get to CVH. I said I would ask my dad to bring her up when he came to visit.

My dad said he would give her a ride and about a week later they came to visit me.

The day they came was a bright sunny day and was kind of warm for March. We went to the side of Battell where there was a picnic table and sat talking and drinking the coffee my dad had bought.

Linda said, "They did a remarkable job on your face, Ted."

I answered, "There is still much work to be done but, thank you. I told her that she wasn't the cause of what had happened and that I was planning to tell her I wouldn't be seeing her anymore."

She said, "I was going to tell you the same thing, Ted."

They visited for about an hour when my dad said, "We have to be leaving, Ted."

I said, "Linda, take care of yourself and it was nice to see you."

She answered, "Good luck with everything. I am sure it will work out for you. Good-by Ted."

The Grand Jury

In the late evening after everyone else was in bed I would sit in the smoking room enjoying the peace and quiet. I would gather my thoughts and would think about the next stage of my court case, the Grand Jury Hearing which was coming up the following week. I prayed for strength to endure whatever the future held for me.

The following week the sheriffs came and transported me to the courthouse.

At the courthouse I was put inside one of the holding cells. As I sat there waiting to be taken up to the court room, I noticed writing on the walls and ceiling put there by other prisoners. Most of the writing stated how much time the prisoner had received for their crime. The sentences ranged from months to life. I wondered what mine might say.

I waited two hours before I was finally taken up to the court room. My attorney said, "It's going to be awhile before the proceedings start."

As I sat there, I looked to my right and saw my in-laws and I saw a police officer whom I learned was the officer I spoke with on the phone the night of the shooting. He was also the officer who put the handcuffs on me and sat me in a chair until the ambulance had arrived.

The judge finally came into the court room and the jury took their seats. The judge said to the jury, "It is your duty to determine if there is enough evidence to bring the defendant to trial; it is not your duty to try the case. Is that understood?"

The jurors answered, "Yes"

Once the jurors went into the jury room my attorney requested to attend the session. His request was denied.

I was taken into the jury room. I sat in a chair that was set on a platform a little higher than the main floor. The jurors were seated in front of me, and the witnesses sat in a chair on the main floor.

The first witness was my mother-in-law. She handed the chairperson a letter I had written her when I was in the medical hospital. The chairperson read the letter to the rest of the jurors. The letter read, "I am sorry for telling you on the phone that Patty had died that night and I have asked the court to allow you to have custody of Michael and Rene. I have asked this because I feel you have suffered enough from my mistake. And I hope the children will bring you all some comfort." The chairperson then handed the letter to the sheriff who presented the letter to the judge who entered the letter as evidence for trial.

My mother-in-law then said, "Ted tried to kill Patty one other time before in their car." I quickly interrupted and said, "Patty and I had been out drinking and we began to argue, and I was driving much faster than I should have and came close to having an accident. I never at any time tried or wanted to kill Patty, including the night of the shooting."

My mother-in-law had no other evidence to present, and they called in the police Sgt to give his testimony.

He sat down and gave the sequence of events. He showed photographs of the crime scene and the shotgun. One of the jurors asked, "What is this thing on the end of the barrel of the shotgun?"

He answered, "That is called a poly choke, and it is used for different types of hunting."

At this time, I began to break down and said, "I can't stay in here any longer, I want to leave."

The sheriff informed the judge of my request, which he granted, and I was taken downstairs to a holding cell.

It was about an hour later when I was taken back to the court room. I sat at the defendant's table with my attorney. He said, "I think the jurors are having a hard time with this." He also said, "Don't write anymore letters."

I said, "I think the letter helped more than it hurt."

The juries' chairperson asked the judge, "Can the charges be lowered?"

He answered, "The charges can be lowered, and insanity would have to be proven."

The jury went back to the jury room and returned about ten minutes later. They determined that there was enough evidence to bring me to trial.

When the jury left, they had to walk by me. Not one of them looked at me.

My attorney said to me, "Don't worry, next time it will be our day in court."

I said to him, "I want to be tried by a three-judge panel."

He agreed it was the best way to go with this.

That evening after returning to the hospital my mother came to visit me. After we talked about the hearing she said, "I have some good news for you. Your father and I didn't tell you, but we have been in court also. We asked the court for you to have visitation rights with the children. The court approved visitation in the hospital under the supervision of either your father or me."

I asked, "When can we start?"

"How does this Sunday sound?"

"Thank you so much mom."

"Both your father and I will be here for the first visit."

Saturday night I laid in bed, my mind racing with thoughts of what would I say to the kids? Although they were only 2 and 3 years old I knew they would have questions. Especially Michael, he saw my face the night of the shooting. I was going to have to tell them that I wouldn't be there with them, that they would come to see me every month.

The reality of how I changed the course of so many lives in one tragic event was overwhelming. I had very little sleep this night.

Sunday morning, I was sitting in my spot against the wall in the hallway where I could look out through the front doors of the lobby. It would still be a couple of hours before they would arrive.

At least two hours had passed when I saw my mother's and then my father's cars pull into the parking circle in the front of the building.

I couldn't bring myself to go out to meet them; I stayed where I was until they came in. My mom was carrying Rene and my dad was carrying Michael. Both of the kids were facing away from me when my dad said, "Michael here is your dad." When Michael turned to face me, he had a very frightened look on his face, as if to see the same last image he had seen of me. He looked my face up and down, and then puckered his lips to give me a kiss. I will never forget that moment as long as I live. I kissed him and then turned to Rene and gave her a kiss also. I took both of them in my arms and just held them in my arms until they became too heavy for me to hold. I said to them, "I love you."

They each answered with, "I love you, daddy.

It didn't take long before their attention turned to the people and things going on around them. They were totally fascinated with the hospital but were even more curious about the other patients and the way they acted. They had a million questions about them.

I brought them into the canteen to buy them a soda and candy. We sat at a table, and they intently watched the patients that to them were acting very strange. The kids would ask, "Why does he do that, or what is she doing?" I explained the best I could, telling them, "They just do and think things differently than us. They can't help it.

The visit lasted for a couple of hours, during which their mother was not mentioned. I was kind of glad of this because I really didn't know what I could tell them if she came up in a conversation.

As they drove off, they were looking out the rear window waving good-by to me.

After they had driven away, I felt very emotionally drained and realized we would never be a whole family as before.

That evening I skipped dinner and went outside to be alone. It was a very chilly evening, so I went to the side of the building where there was a metal grate on the ground. I used to sit or lay on this grate because down inside it there was an exhaust fan that blew out warm air. I would spend many hours on this grate in cold weather over the next seven years.

As I sat there, I pondered the thoughts of, "Was living going to be worth it. Nothing will ever be the same." Part of me wanted to die and part of me wanted to stick it out.

I look back now and wish I knew what I know now; that I wasn't alone, the Lord was there with me, never to leave me nor forsake me. He was there waiting for me to seek Him.

I can see now how He was with me all the way up to the time when I learned through a Christian staff member at an apartment program who Jesus really is; of course, He is the savior which, if that is all He is, is more than anything we deserve and there is no greater gift than the gift of eternal life. But he is so much more. He issued in a new covenant based on better promises. When He ascended, He promised that the

Father would send the comforter, the Holy Spirit who would take up residence in our spirit. We are a new creation and have become the righteousness of God. He will lead us into all truth, to be a present help in time of trouble, a healer and a deliverer. If I had known this my life would have been so much more peaceful during these troubling times.

Oh! How I wish I had a teacher through all those years. How I wish I had read the bible. I could have spent those years in the Word of life instead of trying to fill that void with women, drugs, alcohol and gambling.

For anyone who reads this story and you're seeking to fill emptiness with the things I mentioned you'll never be satisfied. You'll only be putting a band aid on a wound that will never heal until you allow the Master Physician to come into your heart. Jesus can fill any void you have and replace it with peace and forgiveness. He is knocking, waiting for you to allow Him in.

The daily routine went on pretty much the same during the following months so I will from now on jump forward to events and times that I consider pertinent.

A short while after my Grand Jury hearing I sat down with Dr. Johnson, I asked, "What do I have to do to obtain a job here on the grounds?"

"I will put a referral in to the patient employment supervisor, Mary Tagg."

A few days later Mrs. Tagg, (Mary) called me to her office. She asked me, "What type of work are you looking for?"

I asked, "Are there any openings in the canteen?"

"Not at this time, everyone is looking to work in the canteen." She continued, "There is a position on the trucks and there is a position at the print shop, you would like to work with my husband, he runs the print shop."

"I would like the print shop." I answered.

"I'll set up an appointment for you to go over tomorrow morning and speak with him."

The next morning, I walked over to Haviland Hall where the print shop was. I found Mr. Tagg (Carl) sitting at his desk. He was a large man about in his late 50's with gray hair.

"I'm Ted" I put out my hand to shake his.

He said, "You can just call me Carl." He continued, "At this time the hospital is mostly self-sufficient. If something can be done or made at the hospital it is. The hospital has its own fire department, carpenter shop, electrical shop, police department, grounds department, dental office and print shop. Every document or form used in the hospital is printed in this shop. The presses are all offset presses."

I said, "I took two years of printing while I was in trade school but have forgotten a great deal of what I was taught."

"Then it won't be hard to re-teach you", He replied.

I said, "I would like to work with you."

He said, "You can start next Monday at 9:00 am."

"I'll see you Monday morning." I replied.

When I walked into the Lobby of Battell Jim, the one who borrowed my clothes and walked through the snow when we were on ward 83, came up to me and said, "Watch this." He walked up behind Taggy, a severely mentally ill woman who would walk around for hours having conversations with herself, he had a lit cigarette in his hand, and he dropped it into the pocket of her state dress. I watched as she walked around the lobby for about five minutes. The smoke began to come out of her pocket and began to burn her; she started patting her pocket trying to put it out. She was finally able to put it out. I didn't think it was funny, but Jim thought it was hilarious.

I didn't have much of an occasion to speak with Dr. Lee except when I saw him walking to and from work. He lived on grounds just up the street from Battell. One afternoon when he was walking home, I stopped and asked him, "Dr. Lee, is there any possibility of me going to my father's house for the weekend?"

He thought for a moment, then answered, "If I let you go you have to promise that I won't receive and phone calls from the police or prosecutor that you've gotten into trouble."

"I promise."

I was so excited! I ran into the Lobby to the pay phone and called my dad. When he answered I exclaimed, "Dr. Lee said I could go home with you for the weekend! You can pick me up Friday morning and bring me back Sunday."

"Were going to the air show Sunday, would you like to go?"

"Sure, I would. See you Friday morning at nine."

Friday morning finally came, and my dad was on time. He came in and signed me out. On the way we stopped, and he bought coffee for the ride.

When we arrived at his house we went in and talked for a while. Around 11 am I asked, "Can I go upstairs and take a nap?"

He answered, "Of course you can."

I laid in my old bed and thought of how good it felt. Through the afternoon they would call me from time to time, but I just went back to sleep. The next morning my sister came up and woke me. She said, "I never have seen anyone sleep for 24 hours straight before."

I answered, "It felt so good too."

I just hung around Saturday enjoying the peace and quiet and looking forward to the air show the next day.

The next morning, we left for the air show. It was a beautiful sunny day. When we arrived, there were already hundreds of people there.

I remember feeling very nervous and somewhat paranoid. I had thoughts of how easy it would be for someone to come up and stab me. I forced myself to keep my thoughts on the show.

First, they had full scale aircraft go through their maneuvers, then, the part I was really interested in, the radio control models.

Where I was standing there was a rope setup to keep spectators from getting too close. One of the pilots tried to take his model off in a cross wind. As soon as it lifted off the ground the wind caught it and it veered to the right. It was coming directly for me. I put out my hands to stop it, but at the last second it hit the rope and went into the ground about 12 inches from me. My dad said, "That was close! Are you okay?"

"Yes, I am fine." I thought to myself, "Someone is definitely watching over me."

When we returned to the hospital as I was getting out of the car I said to my dad, "Call my in-laws and let them know I had come home for the weekend."

"That may not be a good idea, Ted." But I insisted and he agreed he would.

For some reason I believed they still loved me and understood that the tragedy was not intentional, but I would learn this was not the case.

The next morning, I started my job at the print shop. The work was laid back and Carl was a good teacher and I caught on quickly.

Later that week I was at work when Carl received a phone call. He called me to the phone and said, "Dr. Lee wants to speak with you." I took the call and Dr. Lee asked if I would come over to his office?

When I walked into his office he said, "I received a phone call from the State's Attorney. He was very angry and threatened to have my license taken away if I ever let you leave the hospital again. "How did he find out, Ted?"

"I told my father to tell my in-laws I had spent the weekend with him. I'm sorry I did that now."

"I am not legally able to issue a pass until you are under the hospitals jurisdiction and right now you are under the courts. It may be a couple of years before I can allow you to go home again."

"I understand Dr. Lee. I'm sorry for putting you in a bad position for letting me go home."

The weather was beginning to warm up and I spent much of my time other than work out in the front of Battell sitting on the bench or lying on the grass.

One afternoon while I was sitting on the bench a man came out of Battell carrying a couple of tennis rackets and tennis balls. He was about my height and had a strong build; he had long dark hair past his shoulders and looked to be in his twenties. He walked up to me and asked, "Are you Ted?"

"Yes, I am."

"Hi, I'm Scott. I work with Bob Pickens in recreation. Would you like to go hit a few tennis balls?"

The tennis court was located in back of Woodward Hall and alongside an empty building named Shepard's Hall.

As we walked Scott said, "I have been asked to speak with you, to give you some encouragement. I was also a patient here and was here for two and a half years. My first nine months were spent at Whiting and after my court trial I was transferred here to Battell."

"May I ask why you had been arrested?"

"I was charged with the double homicide of my parents. My psychosis was drug induced. My acquittal was one of the first in CT. I was given zero to 60 years under the

custody of the mental health system. I was released from custody a little over a year ago. The reason I was released so soon is because my psychosis was drug induced and not a chronic mental illness. I'm telling you this to help you have hope concerning your case. Dr. Lee is one of the best forensic psychiatrists in the State if not the country. He'll make sure you're okay."

"Thanks for confiding in me Scott and for the encouragement."

"You're welcome. We will be seeing a lot of each other over your time here."

One afternoon I walked into the lobby and heard a commotion in the front of the supervisor's office. I then saw Paul and two other staff trying to restrain a patient named Elon. They wrestled him to the floor and put a strait jacket on him. There was another staff member, Ralph, lying on the floor and was unconscious. I learned latter that Elon had hit him on the back of his neck and head with a radio. Ralph was out of work from the injury for 6 months and was never the same after that.

Elon was taken to Whiting; he was there for 6 months for the assault. Elon was first committed to the hospital for the homicide shooting of a police officer while he was under the influence of LSD. I will have more to say concerning Elon latter in the story.

One afternoon I was on the ward in the smoking room with 5 or 6 other patients. A new patient had just come down from the locked ward. He was lying on the top of the counter smoking, and he was dropping the ashes onto the floor. It just so happened that my ward work assignment was cleaning the smoking room. I asked him politely, "Would you please use the ash tray."

He answered, "F*** you, I'll kick your ass!"

"You shouldn't underestimate people, no matter how big you may be."

Just outside the door was Mrs. Norton. She heard what was going on and came in and told him to get off the counter and to use the ash tray. When she left the room he said, "I'll see you later."

"Whatever," I answered.

At night as I lay in bed, from time to time I would hear "Ted" and I thought someone had called me but there was no one. This would happen many nights. I thought maybe it was my illness causing it. Then one night I heard it again, "Ted" so I answered "Yes" and then I heard, "What would you have written on Patty's headstone?" I thought for a while and asked, "I would like, Patricia Smith LaPointe, date of birth, date of death, Mother of Michael and Rene." I then went to sleep and didn't think much about it after that and never said anything about it to anyone.

Then the following Mother's Day my mom came to visit me late in the afternoon. My mother made a decision to visit Patty's grave every Mother's Day. We were having coffee in the canteen when she said, "Patty now has a headstone."

I said, "I know what it says on the stone," and told her what it said.

She asked, "How did you know that?"

"God asked me awhile back what I would like on it, and I told him."

I didn't understand anything about hearing the Lord's voice until many years later when I was reading in the bible the book of Samuel the Prophet. Samuel was living with the Priest and one night he heard someone call his name, just like I did, and he went to the Priest's room and said, "You called me, Master."

"I did not call." Samuel went back to bed and again he heard, "Samuel." He asked the Priest again and this happened again, and the Priest finally said to Samuel, "I perceive it was the Lord. Go back to bed and if He calls again say, yes Lord."

This confirmed to me that it was the Lord I heard. I only remember hearing his voice verbally one other time. Mostly when he speaks to me it is through my spirit sort of like a thought that comes to me.

I had now been working at the print shop for about a month and it wasn't a bad job at all. When the press was running there wasn't much to do so Carl and I would sit around drinking coffee. Both Carl and his wife Mary were not in the best of health but were always in the best of spirits.

The second time my children came to visit me they seemed to be more at ease with me and the other patients. Michael had brought his glove and ball. He asked, "Dad could you throw me some pop-ups?"

"Can you catch already? Your only four years old."

We walked over to the empty parking area, and I threw him an easy lob. He caught it. I then threw him a much higher pop-up and it went a little too far. He had to back up and he backed up until he tripped on the curb where the parking lot met the grass. He fell back and as he was falling, he reached out and still caught the ball. I yelled, "Hey Mike you can catch!"

Rene was still only two and wouldn't turn three until July. She spent most of her time with her grandmother. They would sit on the bench talking.

When it was time for the canteen to open, she would ask to go buy something. She would ask question after question about the other patients. She was very fascinated with them and not in a judgmental way either.

After the kids left, I went into the dining room for dinner. I and a number of the other patients would always save a couple of pieces of bread to feed to the pigeons that were always waiting out in front of Battell on the roof. They knew it was time for their evening dinner. We would get them to come right to our feet and then we would try to catch them. Sometimes we got lucky and would catch one. When we did, they would actually eat out of our hand as we held them.

One evening a pigeon got run over by a car and its insides were coming out, but it was still alive. I went inside to get a bag and was going to kill it and put it somewhere, but when I got back outside it was gone. Norm had killed it. I asked, "Did you have to snap its neck?" He wouldn't answer me, he just shook his head. It really troubled him to have to do that.

One afternoon my dad called and said the Veterans Hospital had called and made me an appointment to see the dentist to get a partial plate fitted. I do not know why they would give me a denture but not do my surgery, but I was grateful for anything they could do for me. The transportation had been arranged with Battell. I was to go in two days. I was looking forward to the ride but not about seeing the dentist.

When I arrived at the VA I had to register. They gave me an ID card and I was to bring it for any future appointments.

The dentist did a thorough exam of my mouth. He decided to pull two teeth, one on the bottom and my one and only top front tooth which was loose and abscessed. After he pulled the teeth, he made a mold for an upper plate. He said it would be impossible to make a bottom partial due to not having a jawbone and my gums were gone. I was to return in a week to get it fitted and take it with me.

The day before I was to begin work in the canteen Mary Tag had me come to her office. She said, "I spoke with Mr. Wilson, and he would like to speak with you today about your duties in the canteen. He will be in the canteen at one pm. Will you go and speak with him?"

"Yes, I have seen him there but never spoke with him. I will be there at one."

Mr. Wilson was a large man almost completely bald, and he always wore a suit and smoked cigars. He would come to the canteen every workday to take the money from the day before and to check the inventory, always making sure there was enough of everything the canteen served.

I was waiting outside the canteen door at 1 pm which is when the canteen opens for the afternoon. Ken, the patient canteen manager opened the canteen and I said, "Hey, Ken. I am supposed to meet Mr. Wilson here at this time. I will sit at a table until he arrives."

A few minutes later Mr. Wilson came in the door that enters the canteen in the back of the counter. He was dressed as always in his black suit, and he had a black hat on. I wondered why he always wore black, and I learned he was a minister, but never spoke about God. I wondered why but never asked him.

Ken motioned for me to come behind the counter. Mr. Wilson sat at the small table behind the counter. Mr. Wilson asked Ken, "Can you get us a cup of coffee? Hi Ted, I am Mr. Wilson. So why would you like to work here in the canteen?"

"It seems like a good way to pass some of my time during the day and I like to be busy as much as possible. We have a lot of nothing to do time here at Battell."

"Mary says you were a good worker at the print shop and would make a good canteen worker. I will start with your duties first. The candy shelves and chip racks need to be kept full at all times. Ken will show you how to replace the soda canisters and the CO2 canisters. The refrigerator is also to be kept full with the diet soda. In the freezer are the sandwiches, Ken will show you how to place them in the light oven and how long to heat them up. The most important duty is to learn how to cash in at the beginning of your shift and out at the end of it. You take all the time you need to learn it correctly. You will be working in the morning from eight to eleven; you'll be working with Ken"

"I'm looking forward to working for you and I'll do my best."

"I'm sure you will, Ted. I'll see you in the morning."

At the end of my first morning working, I met a man named Joe. He was the canteen janitor. He cleaned the tables and mopped the floor. Joe was a heavy smoker, and I would give him smokes when I had them and I would also buy him the Eric cigars which we sold in the canteen.

Joe also was diagnosed with schizophrenia, and he heard voices constantly. So much so that he would stop in the middle of what he was doing and begin to scream at the voice he was hearing, actually having a loud verbal conversation with them.

I met a man named Rich who worked the afternoon shift in the canteen. We became good friends over the next couple of years. He was about 21 years of age and was a short man with a slim build. He was acquitted of a first-degree assault against his mother brought on by drugs and was given zero to ten years.

One morning when I was working a large man and a woman came to the counter and asked, "Do you smoke pot?"

I answered, "No." I wasn't going to answer yes to someone I didn't know.

He said, "My name is Arnie, and this is my wife, Judy. I just got off of ward 83 and am now on ward 82." They bought a coffee and left the canteen.

After closing I went out to the front of the building. Arnie was standing by the doors. I asked, "Where is your wife?"

"She went home." He then asked, "Do you want to get high? My wife just brought me a dime bag. I don't like getting high alone."

I took a chance and answered, "Okay." We took a walk and smoked a joint.

Arnie was about six feet tall and weighed over 300 pounds, had sandy brown hair and blue eyes. His wife, Judy was a tall woman and had bright red hair.

I learned from talking with him that he was committed to the hospital for a bank robbery he committed. He had already served ten years in prison for a previous bank robbery.

Arnie was a very good con-artist and when it came to money, he would go out of his way to make it, including stealing it. The police never found the money he stole from the bank and that is probably why he always had money after his wife would visit.

He was of Jewish decent and in no way believed in Jesus which bothered me a little.

He would try to convince me, without success, that Jesus' mother, Mary, and Joseph,

Mary's husband to be when she had conceived by the Holy Spirit, that they had sex and that was how Jesus was born. I didn't argue with him I just continued to believe what I knew was the truth; that Jesus was the son of God.

Arnie, Norm, myself and a man named Cat, a little about Cat, he was a full-blooded Italian with jet black hair and at times he grew his jet-black beard. He was short about 5 ft. 9 in. tall. He was an educated man who came down with schizophrenia. He had some very far out believes about certain scientific facts and he could almost convince you they were true, anyway the four of us spent many hours in the canteen playing a card game called setback. We had a lot of fun doing this and it passed time, which was our goal.

It was now June and during the summer months Bob and Scott from recreation would take some of the patients camping at Harkness Park. Harkness was a State Park for the handicapped located on the edge of Long Island sound.

Bob asked me, "Ted would you like to go with us?"

"I would love to go, but I need to find someone to cover the canteen for me. I'll get back to you."

Later that day I asked Rich to cover for me, he said he would.

The camping trips were from Friday morning till early Saturday afternoon. First thing Friday morning we would go the rear of the kitchen and pick up the food for the trip. Then we would load all the tents

and sleeping bags.

Trip to the State Park took about one hour. Inside the park there were a number of cabins, and the park was only open to the handicapped.

We drove down to the beach where we would spend the night and set up the tents. There were picnic tables under a roofed area. The grills were set up along this area, there was a bathhouse with toilets and showers. The best part was we had all this area to ourselves.

The two staff, Bob and Scott, started the grill while Arnie and myself walked over to a mansion that was noted for its gardens. When I saw them, I understood why. We then went back for lunch.

The lunch consisted of hamburgers, hot dogs, potato and macaroni salad.

After lunch I went for a swim. After my swim I asked Bob, "How far are we allowed to walk?" He smiled and answered, "To the ends of the earth, Ted."

Arnie and I headed down to the end of beach. At the end of the beach there was a wall of rocks with a path that led to another beach. This was the public beach. At the end of this beach there was a creek that emptied into the sound. We did not know how deep it was and did not want to get our wallets cigarettes wet. So, we returned to camp.

Back at camp I told Bob and Scott what we had found. Bob said, "sometimes the creek is ankle-deep and sometimes waste deep, depending on the tide. After supper we will walk over and try to cross it."

Supper that evening was stuffed peppers that were in a tin pan that Bob put on the grill for about an hour. It tasted pretty good.

After we ate, we headed for the creek and Ocean Beach which is an amusement park. At the creek Bob crossed first, it was ankle-deep. On the other side was the boardwalk; it was a good half mile in length.

We walked to where the main concession stands were located. There were ice cream stands, hot food stands and then we found a bar that only serves beer.

We told Bob we would meet him back at camp; he knew exactly what we were up to but didn't say a word.

Arnie, Bob the patient and I went to the bar where we stayed till 10 PM when it closed.

While we were there Bob told us about his captains' pie, which was money the government owes him for his spy missions around the world. He said that if the government had let him North Vietnam would not be there today.

On the way back I was concerned about what Bob and Scott might say, but at the campsite Bob was already in his sleeping bag and Scott was over the fire.

As we sat around the fire, I noticed a tin coffee pot at the edge of the fire. I asked Scott, "Is that coffee?"

He answered, "That's hobo coffee." I poured myself a cup; it tasted better than home coffee on a stove.

We sat around the fire until 2 AM when Scott asked, "Do you guys want to smoke a joint?" Arnie said, "I have been wanting to ask you that all night." They both pulled one out and we passed them around. Then Scott and Arnie went to bed. But I stayed up drinking coffee and smoking cigarettes until 5 AM when Bob, the staff member, Got up.

I asked Bob, "Can you show me how to make hobo coffee?" He said, "Sure, just fill the pot with water, pour the coffee in and put it on the fire. Let it come to a boil, then bring the pot down to the water and set the pot the water. The shock of the cold water draws all the grounds to the bottom of the pot. Then just keep it warm." My first pot came out as good as his.

I asked Bob, "Do you want a cup of mine?" He said, "as soon as I come back from my swim." Bob, so I learned, went for a swim first thing every Saturday morning on the trips. After his swim he had a cup of coffee and then started breakfast.

Breakfast consisted of eggs, however you wanted them, bacon and sausage. He also kept the grill going until everyone ate.

We returned to the hospital around 11:30 AM. I helped unpack and then thanked Bob and Scott. I was looking forward to going every other weekend.

I spent the rest of the day on the grass in front of the building with Norm. Arnie had gone home with his wife and would return Sunday.

That night after supper I was feeding the pigeons and decided to try and catch one. I took the pieces of bread and through them in front of me, a little closer with each piece until the pigeon was between my legs. Then I went for him and caught him. Then I tried to feed him while I held him

That evening my brother, Keith, came to visit. We drove up to the college where he brought out the pot; I knew what was going to happen. But being paranoid, for some unknown reason was, if not better, at least an escape from this emotional pain that never seemed to leave me.

We drove back to Battell and went into the canteen where I got each of us is soda. It was 8 PM by then, but Keith always stayed until 9 PM.

We sat outside talking about old times. Most of the conversation was a bow my 1964 Lemans that a friend of mine built; it was one of the fastest cars around.

From time to time, we would talk about Patty and the things all of us use to do. The talk always made me sad; I guess that was because I knew I would never have those kinds of times again.

That night, upstairs on the ward, I went into the smoky room; everyone was already in bed. I was sitting there enjoying my cigarette when the guy that I had words with a bout throwing ashes on the floor. He came and stood in front of me and said, "I would love to kill you!" I said to him, "We are alone now and if we start throwing hands there is no one here to help you." He started talking junk to me. I said, "All you can do is talk junk." He drew back his hand and before he could hit me, I punched him twice in the chest. I could have punched him in the face if I had wanted to.

A staff member came in and asked," What is going on?" I said, "We are just fooling around." He said, "Well keep the noise down!"

The guy never talked junk to me again.

I felt nervous from the confrontation and knew I would not be able to sleep right away.

I sat up in the smoking room until 3 AM. While I was sitting there, I was thinking about how I have changed since I was a child. The biggest change was when I was drafted into the United States Marine Corps. Before then I was very passive and would avoid any kind of arguments or confrontations. I had only been two fights growing up.

Upon returning home from my service, I would not hesitate or back down from an argument or confrontation.

The Marines extensive combat training gave me courage like I never knew before. They instilled so much aggression in me that I couldn't wait to get into a fight. Then after they trained me for combat, they never sent me to do what they trained me to do.

I brought all that hostility home with me and took it out on innocent people, including my family.

Then when the schizophrenia kicked in, I was a stick of dynamite just waiting to go off. When it did it cost my wife her life and almost my own.

The next morning while I was working in canteen with Ken, he said, "I am going to be discharged in about a week and I'm going to ask Mr. Wilson to promote you to the manager position if you want the job." I answered, "If Mr. Wilson is willing, I will accept to promotion. Thank you for your support

When Mr. Wilson came in Ken asked him," Can I speak with you?" Mr. Wilson turned to me and asked me to go pick up the change for the day. This was the first time he had ever asked me.

When I returned asked, "Did you have any problems?" I said, "No."

He asked me to sit down and then said, "I'm impressed with your work, and I agree you are the best person for the management position.

Do you have any idea how long you will be here?" I answer, "I will be here for a very long time, Mr. Wilson." He said, "I'm not happy you have to stay, but on the other hand it is difficult to find someone who is both reliable and will be here for more than month or two. The job is yours."

The duties of being the manager were the same except I had to make sure all the shifts were covered, even if that meant covering them myself. I also had to manage all the money.

Rich took over the morning shift and we hired a man named Bob R who was willing to work the weekends so I could go on the camping trips.

Bob was a large who stood 6' 4" tall and weighed a good 240 pounds. He was an active alcoholic who loved his whiskey. He would make a trip down the hill to the package store once a day and by 2 pints to get through the day. From time to time, I would have a shot with him.

Remember the young guy, Jim, he is the one who walked through the snow to another building to see friends?

Well, he went AWOL and stole a car from a dealership. The car had a gun in it, and he returned to the hospital to pick up a guy who came from Whiting. After he picked him up, they went over to another building to pick up a woman. I guess they were seen because a security guard stopped them in a hallway. The guard was wrestling with the both of them and Jim kept telling the other guy to pull a gun. By that time more staff came to help.

Jim went to jail and the other guy went back to Whiting. I never saw Jim again.

After that incident the hospital police requested to be able to carry weapons. They were denied.

One morning I was finishing the shift with Rich. I saw Joe cleaning behind the counter, and he took a pack of Eric cigars. When I told him to put it back, he became very angry and was talking under his breath. I asked, "What are you going to do, Joe? He answered, "I'll kick your ass!"

I believed he would too, and I realized a pack of cigars was no big deal. At least not getting my ass kicked for it.

One afternoon I was standing outside when Louie, the young man that I knew since he was a kid and visited with my family on Ward 83 had his T-shirt inside out. I said, "Louie your T-shirt is inside out, turn it around." I must have told him four times, when he finally turned it around; I couldn't believe my eyes. The shirt was completely dirty. I said, "So that's why, huh Louie? He turned it back inside out.

I called my mom one afternoon and asked," Are you coming tonight?" She answered, "I am." I asked, "Do you know if Johnny has any pot?" She said, "I will check his room." I said, "Just bring enough for a couple of joints."

That evening when she came, I asked her, "Were you able to bring some?" She took out a baggy that had close to an ounce in it. Not only did she bring the pot she brought a six pack of beer too.

My mom, Arnie and I sat in the car. Arnie and myself did not smoke any pot because my mother doesn't smoke, and I didn't want her to have to smell it. But we drank the beer.

Fourth of July came around and the recreation stuff was going to bus anyone who wanted to go see the fireworks to a baseball field in town. Arnie went home on pass for the day. Ralph, Norm, Bob R, Bob K, Rich, and I went. The town put on a good display.

It was time to see the kids again and this time Michael brought his baseball bat. The three of us played outside until I became tired. I went inside to talk with my mom, but I made sure I could watch the kids through the window.

Michael was hitting acorns with the bat when Rene got a little too close and Michael swung the bat and hit her on the forehead. She came running in crying. It was not a bad cut but would need a couple of stitches.

While I was checking your head Michael kept saying to me, "It was an accident, daddy." I said, "I know Michael, don't be nervous. You're not in any trouble."

I brought her into the supervisor's office where they cleaned the cut and my mom had to bring her to the ER which was less than a mile away to get stitches.

Michael stayed with me. They were gone about two hours and when they returned it was past time for them to go home. We said goodbye.

I was getting impatient waiting for my trial. I asked Arnie, "What can I do to get my trial over with?" He said, "You can write to the judge and tell him you want your day in court." We sat down and wrote a letter to the judge who was on the bench at that time. The one and only "Judge Sadin," whose nickname was Satan. I requested he send me to trial.

The next morning, I mailed it and then called my attorney and told him about the letter. He became furious and said, "If you don't retract that letter, I am going to refuse to represent you."

I was able to get the letter before it went to the hospital post office.

Every summer each of the buildings had a building picnic. They were held about 2 miles away at a place called Hemlock Grove. It was State land, and it was set back about a quarter mile in the woods. The entire area around it was beautiful, with a couple of lakes and hiking trails.

The morning of the picnic a few of us chucked the corn.

We were then bused out to the picnic site where the staff already had the fires going.

There was enough food to feed an army; burgers, hot dogs, corn on the cob, macaroni salad, potato rolled salad and steak was for supper.

One afternoon I was working with Rich in the canteen when Norm, who is playing setback, called over to look at his hand. I could not believe what I saw; he had the most perfect hand you get in setback. It was like getting a Royal Flush in poker. It was the first and only time I have ever seen one.

The middle of September 1977 rolled around, and it was time for the last camping trip of the year. There was only three of us who wanted to go; Arnie, Bob K and myself.

On the way to the park, we stopped and all of us chipped in for steaks. I also bought batteries for my radio.

The weather was too cold to sleep outside so Bob arranged for us to use a trailer.

Although the weather was chilly it didn't stop Bob from going swimming. I also went in the water myself; believe me the water was cold. After swimming we went back to have our steaks.

About six that evening we became tired of hanging around the trailer, so we decided to drive over to Ocean Beach. It was too cold to cross to creek; that's why we drove.

We walked around the boardwalk for all the concession stands were closed. We decided to take a ride to a store to buy soda and chips and spend the evening inside the trailer. It wasn't one of the better camping trips.

One morning I was looking out the window from the canteen. I thought to myself," I would like to see it snow." Although it was only October, October 13 to be exact.

The very next day 2 inches of snow fell. The leaves were still on the trees, and I said in my thoughts, "Thank you God!"

Most of the patients looked forward to the holiday season; this is when the hospital held parties and had special meals.

Well, I was happy for the holidays, but it also was the first anniversary of the shooting. I did my best not to dwell on this. But rather tried to focus on Thanksgiving. In a way this Thanksgiving was special to me because I was going to eat solid turkey if it killed.

On Thanksgiving Day, we went to the dining room two words time. All the tables were covered with tablecloths, and they had all the walls covered with decorations.

I went through the line and had them fill my plate with turkey, turnips, mashed potatoes and the best part sausage stuffing, which I asked for more of, but they would not give me extra.

I went and sat at a table with Arnie, Ralph, and Norm. We talked and laughed about me eating the meal. It took forever for me to eat the meal, but I ate everything on my plate.

Not much happened from Thanksgiving to the middle of December when my birthday rolled around. My mom, dad, brothers, and sisters came to visit me, but not all at the same time, which was good because my whole day was filled with family members at different times.

After the last of them had left I went to my ward and sat in the smoking room to calm down. I was overwhelmed by all the attention; I finally went to bed at midnight.

On December 23, my one-year anniversary in the hospital was also the day for the building to have their Christmas party. It started in the dining room with a prime rib dinner. It was nice because the staff waited on the tables.

It wasn't easy for me to eat to meat; but I managed just fine.

After the meal the party began. It started in the lobby where there were tables with different kinds of chips and dips. From 6 to 8 PM. At eight the dancing began in the auditorium.

Paul from Ward 83 had at that time, a band mostly made up of staff members; they were very good.

At 9 PM Santa came around and gave out gifts. The party ended at 10 PM. It was a nice change from the daily routine.

YEAR TWO

On Christmas Day my brother Keith and his fiancée Cathy came to visit me. They did not stay long; they had people to go see.

Later that day my mother came; she brought me a carton of cigarettes and gave me some money. She stayed a couple hours and then had to leave.

My father was not able to come, he had too much to do.

One evening just after New Year's I asked the nurse on the second shift if I could get something for headache. She started to yell at me saying, "you're just going to have to wait awhile!" I asked another staff member, "What's wrong with her?" The staff member said, "Don't take it personally; she just finished giving CPR to a woman patient who hung herself in the bathroom. The woman died."

Later that evening the nurse came with medicine for my headache. She said, "I'm sorry for the way I spoke to you Ted." I answered, "I understand."

One morning when the canteen first opened a patient named Alfonse asked Rich for a cigarette. Rich said, "You still owe me a pack. When I get what you owe me then I'll give you one." Alfonse yelled out, "You see that guy, he tried to kill his own mother!" Rich picked up a chair; that was made of wood and threw it. Alfonse caught it just as it his chest; he threw it to the side. They both met in the center of the canteen. They both started talking junk to one another, "Let's get it on, let's get it on!" For a few seconds I thought there was going to be a hell of a fight. But neither of them would throw the first punch. They just kept talking junk. Someone must have gone to the supervisors' office because a minute later the supervisor came in and asked, "What's going on here?" I said to her, "They just had an argument, that's all." When the supervisor left Alfonse went back to his seat and Rich left the canteen.

Nothing happened eventful for the next couple months. February came and went. It was sometime in March that a new woman came to Battell. Her name was Linda; she wasn't a bad looking woman. She was about 5'4" tall with black hair and dark eyes.

She introduced herself to me and we started to spend a lot of our past time together. I did not feel like there was anything between us, except for being friends and having someone, other than the guys, to speak to.

Then one afternoon I was taking a nap on a bench near the auditorium when she came in and kissed me and then walked away. I followed her outside and asked her, "Why did you kiss me?" She answered, "You looked cute laying there."

It was then that we started to become sort of a couple.

I explained to her why I was there and how I was going to go to trial sometime in the near future.

She told me she just went through a divorce and was in the process of selling her home.

She kept telling me she wanted to sleep with me. I explained to her that the medication I was taking caused me to have ED. And also, I wasn't ready for that.

The weather was getting warmer, and I had known Linda for over a month now. One afternoon I said to Linda, "I can't wait to get my surgery done so I can get this tube out of my throat."

She said, "I thought that was some kind of necklace or something."

It was nearing the end of April and the weather was warm enough to go camping again. But because Bob was on vacation we would not go to the beach. Instead, we would go with another rehab staff member, named Ted, and we were going to Hemlock Grove near the lakes.

That evening out at the grove Linda and I were going to walk off somewhere and make love. But the staff member kept a close eye on us, and we were unable.

The beginning of May came around and my brother, Keith, and Cathy's his fiancé were going to be married.

I asked Dr. Lee if I could attend the wedding? He said he could not allow me to go.

I did not like that answer, so I spoke with Keith about having a couple friends pick me up and take me to the wedding. it would have worked if I could get back by 9 PM.

We decided to try it, but my father got wind of it and would not let us do it.

It turned out that I was lucky because the Judge that was to marry them was one of the Judges that was going to be on my panel of judges at my trial. Talk about the blessing of God!

The day of the wedding came and although I could not go, I decided to celebrate anyway. I walked down the hill to the package store and bought a bottle of gin. When I got back to the building, I hid it in the canteen.

Linda was gone for the weekend with her parents, so I decided to drink alone. I drank it late that afternoon. What I didn't expect was that my mom and her best friend, Eve, coming to visit me.

We sat in the lobby, and I was pretty drunk. I was getting very loud, and the supervisor came out and asked me," What is wrong?" I said to her, "What is you shut the hell up!"

The next thing I knew was four staff members around me. One of them, Ron, said, "Ted you have to come with us." I said, "Sure."

They took me up to ward 83 and were going to put me in the isolation room. I wanted no part of that and started to resist. They brought me down and put me in a strait jacket and put me on a bed. A short while later I had to vomit; I turned my head and let it go, all over the floor.

One of the staff members cleaned it up.

They took me out of the jacket an hour later. I slept through the night.

I spent the rest of the weekend on the locked ward. Monday morning Dr Lee came on the ward with another doctor. I heard Dr. Lee say to him, "Ted's brother just got married and he was unable to attend the wedding. Otherwise, I would never do this." He called me over and said, "Ted, I will let you go back to the open ward, but you have to promise to never do this again." I answered, "I promise."

I was returned to the open ward.

THE TRIAL

It was now the beginning of June 1978 when one afternoon Dr. Lee was leaving to go home for the day that he stopped me outside the front of the building and said, "Ted, the court called me today and said you will be going to trial next week. Try not to be worried, I think everything will work out."

I appreciated him trying to tell me not to worry but I was a bundle of nerves for that entire week.

The day before I was to go to trial, I woke up early and went out on my pass. That entire day I paced around and around the front of the building. A bout 4 PM Dr. Lee was leaving to go home. One of the other patients was speaking with him when he saw the coming over to him. He said to the patient, "I will speak with you later, right now I need to speak with Ted."

He said to me, "Ted, I have no doubts about how it is going to turn out. Try to stay calm. If you need a little extra medication, I will order a PRN for you." I said, "I think I do need something." He said, "I will call in the order."

The medication helped me sleep through the night.

The next morning, I was in the lobby waiting for the sheriffs to arrive. They arrived at 9:15 AM and on came the cuffs.

At the courthouse I was put in the holding cell. I wait there for about an hour before I was up to the court room.

When I walked into the court room, I could not believe how many people were there! I tried not to look as I walked over to the table where my attorney was standing.

A few minutes later the three judges came in and sat on the bench.

The court was called to order. The first witness called to testify was the police Sgt. he testified that he received a call that there was a shooting at my residence. He testified that he spoke with me on the phone.

They then passed around photos to the judges, prosecutor and my attorney. I did not look at the photos. One of the judges asked the Sgt. "Is this where they found the weapon?" The Sgt. answered, "Yes, it is."

It was on the dining room table. My attorney asked, "Was it a serious attempt to take his life?" The Sgt. answered, "A very serious attempt."

The next person to testify was Dr. Lee. He testified that I was out of contact with reality when shooting occurred. He stated that I was paranoid and believed there was an intruder in the house.

One of the judges asked, "Was there any drugs in his system at the time of the shooting? Dr. Lee answered, "The drug screen taken at the hospital states there was no drugs or alcohol in his system."

The next and last person to testify was Dr. Van Dyke the psychiatrist from the medical hospital. He was asked, "What state was he in when you evaluated him?" He answered, "Mr. LaPointe was still at that time very paranoid but showed a great deal of remorse over what had happened. He needs to be hospitalized and medicated for his schizophrenia and will need extensive therapy.

They then rested their case.

The judges left to decide the verdict.

I was taken down to the holding cell. It took about one hour for them to decide.

When they did, I was brought back to the court room.

The Head Judge asked me to stand. He said, "The court finds that the defendant was suffering from a mental disease or defect and is hereby acquitted of the charge of murder. He is to be commented to the State hospital not to exceed 90 days.

I felt like a ton of weight had been taken off my shoulders.

I thanked him and then I was brought down to the holding cell. About one hour later I was transported back to the hospital.

Back at Battell I went to Linda's ward and told her, "I was acquitted." She gave me a big hug and said, "Now it's time for you to start a new life, Ted."

Dr. Lee called me into his office, he said, "Ted, now that your trial is over, I have the authority to grant you passes to go home with your family." I asked, "When can they start?" He answered, "How about this weekend?" I said, "Thank you Dr. Lee, for everything."

The weekend passes with my mom and dad went well. On the weekends that I saw my children I would stay back at the hospital.

On one of my passes with my dad we sat down and filled out forms for my Social Security disability

I was denied three times. All three times I appealed their decision.

A little more than a year later I was to go before a Law Judge, but before that happened, I went into the VA hospital for my surgery.

SURGERY

Some time that July I went to the VA hospital in West Haven CT. where I thought I would be for a few moments. It turned out that I was there for close to a year.

I was put on the surgical ward, fourth floor, building one.

About four days after I was admitted I had to go before a panel of doctors. There must have been seven

all of them, each taking turns looking at my chin and inside my mouth. A doctor, named Dr. Polayes,

was going to be the chief surgeon in charge of the surgery.

There was an intern, but I can't remember his name.

They sat there talking for a while using medical language I never heard before.

They decided they would start in a couple of weeks.

The nurses on the surgical ward were very kind and laid back. I spent most of my time walking around learning the layout of the hospital inside and outside.

Linda had discharged from CVH, and she came to visit me. She asked me, "Ted can you get out on here for a couple of hours to go to dinner, my treat?" I said, "They won't even know that I am gone. But first I have to get my street clothes." We decided to go in two days.

Later that day I talked the nurse into getting my clothes out of storage.

Linda came two days later to pick me up. She took me to a restaurant on the water and she treated me like a king.

We had a nice dinner and talked for about an hour. She then told me, "I am not going to see you anymore. My parents said if I continue to see you, they will not help me. They feel you have too much going on in your own life to be involved in my life also."

I said, "I can totally understand that, and I want you to know that I appreciate your kindness and understanding. Maybe someday things will be different."

We never saw one another again.

One afternoon my mother's best friend, Evy, came to visit. I asked her, "Can you ask Herb, her husband, if he would go to my moms and pick up my TV? It's too heavy for my mom to carry." She said, "I will have him pick it up and bring it this weekend."

One afternoon I was walking around outside when I thought I smelled pot. I walked around some bushes there was a man there smoking pot. I asked him, "Can I get a hit?" He answered, "Here take this." He gave me a whole joint. I thanked him and he walked off.

There were two main buildings at the hospital, building one and building two. Each had nine floors; I was in building one fourth floor. It was the surgical ward. Between the two buildings there was a walkway connecting the two. There was also a large grassed-in area; a number of benches where people would sit and feed the pigeons.

I would eat my meals in my room, I asked the doctor, "Can I have a beer with my meals?" He said, "I will order you one beer a day."

That didn't matter too much to me because my mom always brought a six pack with her.

I was not supposed to drink alcohol because of the medications I was taking, but I liked one or two because it relaxed me.

I became friends with a nurses aid, his name was John. Every day he would bring me a couple of joints.

One evening I was walking around and decided to check out basement floors. I took the elevator down to the basement. I was amazed at what I found; there were tunnels everywhere. I thought to myself, "This will be a good place to smoke when its bad weather outside." I found that I could walk to other buildings to.

I had been there three weeks now without any work being done on me. Then one afternoon Dr. Polayes came in to see me. He said, "We want to fit you with a plastic mouthpiece to keep your jaw in place after we do the reconstruction. In a couple days we will make it and then will set a day to wire your jaw to hold the mouthpiece in place.

The day for the fitting came and he made the mouthpiece in the med room on the ward. The fitting was made of epoxy; like what you would use to fix something in your home. He put a piece of plastic in my mouth so the epoxy would not burn my gums. Even with the plastic I still felt the heat of the epoxy as it cured.

After it set, he put back in my mouth to see if it was doing what he wanted it to do, which was to keep both sides of my bottom jaw in alignment. He liked the fit.

He said, "In about a week we will do the first stage of your surgery; were going to wire your jaw closed and make your mouth larger." I said, "You're the boss, Dr. Polayes."

It was the third week of August; two weeks longer than he said it would be to do the first stage. The surgery took four hours; I was back in my room when I woke up.

When the nurse came in, she exclaimed, "Wow! I have never seen such swollen lips." I asked, "could I have something for pain?" She came back and gave me a shot of morphine.

In five minutes, I was nodding out. I thought to myself "I love pain medication!"

Later that day I looked in the mirror, she was right, my top lip was very swollen; I was also wired shut and I could tell my mouth had been enlarged. But still I was not satisfied with my mom; it was still small and a normal person, and my bottom lip was not the correct shape.

I later learned from Dr. Polayes that I would need at least two more surgeries after the reconstruction.

I was put on a liquid diet that consisted of soup and ensure. I wasn't aware then that I would be on this diet for many months before my jaw would be unwired.

One Sunday in September my mom brought my children to see me. There was another patient in the room with me who smoked a pipe. My son Michael was watching him and said, "My daddy use to smoke a pipe." I looked at my mom and we both smiled. We both knew the only pipe I smoked was pot.

There was one nurse who didn't care for me; when she gave me my pain injection, she knew just how to stick the needle in so that it hurt. I never gave her the satisfaction of knowing it hurt.

After they stopped the morphine, I asked the doctor for something to help me sleep. He gave me a medication, I don't remember the name, it was a liquid. It worked for a few days; after that it was not effective. I let the doctor know and he ordered a second dose after the first dose. I would always wait for the second dose. For some reason I always needed to feel high; it was the only way I could cope.

It was now the middle of September, and the weather was beginning to get chilly. One evening my brother, Keith, came up to visit with me. He said, "I have some good pot; do you want to get high?" I answered, "That's a silly question; of course, I want to." He said, "You are in your pajamas, and it is too cold to go outside like that. Do you know where we could go?" I answered, "Wait until you check this place out." I took them both down to the tunnels.

While we were smoking out of nowhere, I had this overwhelming urge to go to the bathroom and I could not hold it! I said, "I'm going to go in my pajamas! Before I could finish the sentence it all came out. It went down my legs and on my slippers. I said, "I'm sorry but I could not hold it. I have to go shower." Keith said, "Don't feel embarrassed, that will happen to anyone who has been on a liquid diet for as long as you."

I took my shower and wash my slippers; I thought that would help but the next morning they smelled terribly.

One of the nurses came into the room and could smell the odor. She said, "Someone needs new slippers." I threw the slippers away.

I went down to the store in building two and bought a pair.

I was kind of embarrassed because there was three other men in the room, and they could not help but to smell it. But they never said a word.

One afternoon I requested to see a VA disability representative. When he came to see me, I explained to him that I had schizophrenia and wanted to file for disability. We filled out the forms and assigned them. What I didn't recognize at the time is that he applied for non-service-connected disability. I wanted to file for service connected.

The reason being I believed the Marine Corps training aggravated my schizophrenia. Two weeks later the papers came back; I was denied.

It was a few years later that I filed for service-connected disability. It was 30 years later before I won my claim.

The next couple of months went by. Finally, the time came for my reconstructive surgery to be done. Dr. Polayes came to see me, he said, "We have decided to use a piece of your collarbone and surrounding muscle to shape your jaw. We will also take a piece of bone from your pelvis and graft it into your collarbone. There will be a scar around your neck. Is that okay with you?" I answered, "That will be okay with me."

The evening before they were to perform the surgery the nurse came in and said, "I have to put an IV in your hand, also I have a surprise for you at 10 o'clock tonight."

I had no idea what the surprise could be. When 10 o'clock came, she brought in medication, a Valium and a double dose of sleep medication.

She said, "Good luck tomorrow."

In the morning before I went down to the surgery, they gave me medication to relax me. A short while later I was taken to the operating room. The surgery lasted eight hours.

When I woke up, I was in severe pain; they kept me pumped up with morphine.

There was a drainage tube in my shoulder and also another in my hip. They both fell out after a couple of hours of me moving around. They never replaced them.

A couple of days later I looked in the mirror; I couldn't really tell how it looked due to the swelling. There was also a pin in my shoulder and my arm was in a sling. I was told that I should keep my arm as still as possible. Not me, I took my arm out of the sling as often as possible.

One day as I was watching TV when I heard this loud snap in my shoulder along with a sharp pain. I thought that I just moved my arm the wrong way. But the sharp pain would not subside.

I spoke to the nurse about the pain. She called the doctor, and he ordered an x-ray. After it was taken, I asked if I could see it? The x-ray showed what looked like two pins in my shoulder; what actually happened was the pin had snapped in two. They decided not to take it out is out.

One evening I was sitting on my bed watching TV I had an itch on my shoulder and when I went to scratch it, I noticed that it was oozing pus and when I pressed on the incision a great deal of pus came out.

I was concerned that it might be infected so I told the nurse who notified the doctor who assisted in the surgery, and he came to see me. I showed him how, when I put pressure, on the incision is kept oozing pus.

He, at first, thought it was infected but when he smelled it, he said, "I think it's just drainage. I don't think it's infected; will keep an eye on it."

About a week went by and the discharge of pus had ceased and the only pain I was experiencing was in my hip. If I coughed or laughed, it was very painful.

One morning I went into the nurse's station to say hi; while I was talking to, I felt a sharp pain in my shoulder. When I reached up to grab my shoulder half of the broken pin fell on the floor.

I asked the nurse, "Did you see that?" She said, "Yes I most certainly did. Are you okay?" I answered, "Yes, I think so."

Since that time, I experienced no more pain in my shoulder. But that left the other half of the pin deep in my shoulder. It would be two years before the other half worked its way out.

The assistant surgeon came in to see me and to check on how I was healing. I said, "I am fine except on the bottom of my chin there is an open hole." He looked at it and then took a Q-tip and put it into the hole. It went pretty far into the hole; he then asked, "Can you feel that your mouth?" I answered, "No, I can't feel it." He said, "That's good to hear. I think it will heal on its own."

During the entire healing process, I was receiving morphine injections for pain. My arms looked like pin cushions. She asked, "How about I give this to you in the hip?" I answered, "Okay." She gave me the injection and I said, "That's the last time for that!" Man did that hurt!

One day the nurse came in and asked, "Are you constipated? Because all the morphine you are taking can have that effect." I answered, "A little but it's not too bad."

Well two days later I wasn't able to go, and I was given a laxative.

It was the first week of January when the doctor came in and said, "It's time to take the wires out of your jaw. I'm going to give you your last shot of morphine. I'll be back in 30 minutes to take the wires out."

When he came back, I asked him, "Can you take the trake out also?" He answered, "we can take that out too."

The surgeries came out good but not completely successful. The bone graft did not take. The left and right side of my chin did not grow together, and I can move the left side up and down. Also, my mouth was still smaller than normal.

It would not be until 1997 when I met a plastic surgeon who could repair my jaw. He removed the bone graft and replaced it with a piece of my rib. He used screws to hold it all in place.

He said that the bottom of my tongue was bound to my lower gum. He repaired it and put in skin grafts.

He also put three dental implants in my lower jaw. They were screwed into a metal plate that he put in under the bottom of my jaw. This gave my jaw tremendous strength.

In 2010 the VA paid to have dentures made for me. I have never been able to wear them because they are too uncomfortable; my mouth is just too small inside.

BACK AT BATTELL

My first day back at Battell I ran into Dr. Lee in the hallway. He said, "Ted, meet me at my office, I need to speak with you.

While you were in the hospital the court had a hearing; they sentenced you to 0 to 25 years. But that doesn't mean you will do all 25 years. But it does mean you will be here for some time.

I went back to my duties as the canteen manager. On my first day back, I was given the bad news that Mr. Wilson had passed away.

A young man by the name of Jeff had taken over the position of overseeing myself and the other workers.

Jeff was not a bad man to work for. He was young, handsome, with sandy brown hair and stood about 5'10" tall and the ladies loved him.

We had two canteens to take care of: the one in Battell and the one in Merritt. I handled the duties at Battell and Jeff handled Merritt. I worked for a few hours in the morning at Battell and in the evening, I would run the canteen in Merritt.

The two patient workers that took care of the cleaning were both named Joe. A black man, who I mentioned before, how we had an argument and he said, "I'll kick your ass!" After that I gave more respect, which he rightly deserved. He wasn't as dumb as I thought, or at least wasn't letting on.

The other Joe was a large man who had been a patient, at that time, 20 years. He took care of cleaning Merritt.

Now that my trial was over Dr. Lee said he now had the authority to allow me to go home on the weekends. So, from Friday to Sunday, I was either at my father's home or my mother's home.

Now that I was acquitted, I filed for my Social Security disability. I was denied three times; after the third time I filed for a hearing before a law judge., But before all this happened, I received a phone call from my attorney who was handling my lawsuit. Years before I was employed by a die-casting factory, where I was operating a casting machine and I suffered first second and 3rd° burns over 60% of my body.

This attorney said that he could only get $7000 from the company. Like a fool! I accepted it. After the insurance company received their portion and the lawyer received his portion, that left me with $2500.

Within two weeks I had the money. I asked my mom to find a car and I would let her drive it until I was out of the hospital. (I thought I would get out soon). Her car had gone bad, and she was driving my sister's car. I thought this was the least I could do for her for her faithfulness.

That very week she called and said, "Ted, I have found a car; it is a 68 Cougar, and they want $1800 for it. There is another car that is salesman said would be a good transportation vehicle. He said the Cougar is a good car but needs front end work. I like the cougar. You might not like the color: it is a mustered color."

My mom came down and I gave her $2000 to buy the cougar, that's the one she wanted.

One morning my friend and I went to the cottage to buy breakfast. I couldn't believe what I saw him do! Inside the cottage when you walk in there was a dining room table and on the other side next to the kitchen doorway was a bookshelf. One of the ladies who worked in the kitchen left her pocketbook on the bookcase. I saw him going through the pocketbook; this was right out in the open in front of everyone, there had to be seven people in the dining room. He was so casual about it, no one noticed. He took all the money that poor woman had! I was just as guilty because I like it happen: the truth is I was afraid of them.

Nothing was said about the incident.

Two months after I left the VA hospital my trach had never closed up. I had to go to Middlesex to have surgery to close it up. After it was closed it took a week to heal.

Before it healed, one afternoon I went into the supervisor's office to ask about something as I was speaking there was this high-pitched whistle sound. The supervisor asked, "where is that noise coming from? "I started to laugh and said, "It's coming from my throat!" He looked at me kind of strange, then started to laugh too.

Since I was given permission to visit my children, on the hospital grounds, visits went on with no problems.,

On one visit we decided to drive it around the grounds, which we had permission to do. The grounds covered a large area, and we went by the garage where there were gas pumps.

I guess, when the kids got home, their grandmother asked them what they did with their father? Michael must have told her that we went to a gas station.

She thought we went off grounds. She obtained a court order, saying my mother was unfit to supervise my children.

My mother went to court to fight the restraining order. (My mother, before the shooting, was a supervisor at a training school for the mentally retarded for 12 years; since that time, she cared for terminally ill patients in their homes.) When this evidence was submitted to the court my mother-in-law had nothing to stand on. The visits went on as usual.

My brother Charlie was discharged from the Navy, and he came to visit me with my mother. He drove up in his 67 Mustang. He asked, "Do you want to try it out?" I drove it up to the lake; it ran pretty well! But could not touch my 67 Lemans that I used to have.

My brother Keith continued to come visit me during the week, even though I had weekend passes.

Him and his wife, Cathy, would take me out to the lakes; where we would walk around the woods, and they would take pictures of me. When I saw the pictures, I would laugh because I looked like I was pregnant. It took time to lose that gut; caused by the medication and state food.

Sometime in August we had a new patient come onto the ward. His name was Tom. He was only with us a few weeks. He told me that he lives in a cabin out by the lakes a long side state property.

I was telling him that when I was a young teenager I use to go to a stone query, that was half freshwater and half saltwater. A bunch of us would go there swimming. They say that when digging the quarry, they hit and underground spring; its hundreds of feet deep and they say there are still cranes at the bottom.

He told me how there was a place pass the lakes and alongside the power lines; where people go four wheeling and there is a query. He said it was like the one I told him about, but it was all freshwater. He said that after he gets discharged for me to come to his house and he would take me there. It sounded like fun.

A bout two weeks after Tom was discharged, I asked Keith if he wanted to go and check the place out? We drove out to Tom's house, and we drove to the query in Tom's car. We drove to the power lines where there was a dirt road entrance a long side the power lines. His car was not a four-wheel-drive, so, we parked alongside the dirt entrance.

It was a good mile walk; it didn't bother us because we had all day. A long side the road were raspberry bushes, so we stopped and ate a bunch of them.

As we got near the query, we could hear people laughing and talking; I said, "What a place for a party! We could make all the noise we wanted to and never be heard.

We walked around a curve in the road, and we could see four wheels trucks and a Volks wagon. I said, "How could that get up here?" Tom answered, "They had to come up from the other side; but is still hard to believe he made it.

We walked up to the query's edge where we could see some people swimming. The query was not that big but still had plenty of room. On the other side was a rock ledge where people were jumping off into the water; on our side there was a rope tied to a tree branch, where people could swing out into the water.

The three of us went swimming and one of the guys there gave us each a beer. We stayed here until 7:30 PM and then walked back to the car. Keith said, "We have to get Dave to come up with this four-wheel truck!"

All and all things were going well, at least as good as can be expected, seeing I had to be there.

A new Doctor took charge of our ward. I'll call him Dr. Meany. He told me in no uncertain terms that I belonged in prison and that if he had the choice, I would not have passes.

He was like a snake waiting to strike at me.

I finally received the date for my Social Security hearing. My father and stepmother said they would take; Dr. Lee gave the okay.

The day came and we arrived at the courthouse. While we were waiting my dad asked to see my records? For a good half hour, they read my file.

When we were called into the court room, the first thing the judge asked was, "Can you work?" I answered, "I don't know; I have been confined to the hospital for two years." He asked me to leave the room, that he wanted to speak to my parents. He also said, "Have a happy Thanksgiving."

A short while later they came out and on the way to the car my dad stated, "You will never get the disability, Ted!

Two weeks went by when I received a phone call from my dad. He said, "I have some good news you. You were awarded your disability claim! The judge felt that because of your schizophrenia you are unable to work in a competitive labor group. Also, your disability will commence from the first day you entered the hospital. How does that sound, Ted!" I answered, "That's great news, dad!"

A bout a week went by when I received a letter from Social Security; it is stated that I would not receive back payment as ordered by the court. The reason being is a claim can only go back to the day it was first filed.

So instead of receiving $40,000 I will receive $10,000; that seemed fair to me.

One evening I was sitting in the canteen with my mother, when my father walked in and sat with us. He said, "I have a check for you, it is nowhere near as much as you thought." He handed me the check; it was for $500. I said, "I think this is my monthly check and not the back payment check." It turned out that I was right.

Around this time when the word was getting out that I would be receiving a fair amount of money a young woman kept coming on to me. We ended up being a pair. I will not go into detail about her or our relationship, other than our relationship lasted about a year; she even lived with my mother for a short time. When the money was gone, she was gone.

When I received the retroactive money, I was given permission to attend an auto technician school. I drove there and had to return by 9 PM. The course was one year; I only finished half the course.

This tendency of not finishing what I start, whether it's school or employment has plagued me ever since my last few months in the Marine Corps. It has been determined that these are symptoms of my schizophrenia.

One summer day I was going to go to my mother's, and I asked my friend, Ralph, if you would like to go. He said, "I'd like that; but how will your mother feel about it? I answered, "She won't mind at all. So don't worry about that."

It couldn't have been more than an hour later when the staff calls all patients back to the wards for an emergency meeting.

What I was about to hear was going to blow my mind! The head nurse said that Ralph had jumped off the overpass headfirst onto the highway. He was pronounced dead on arrival.

I went to the funeral and said my goodbyes. He was a good friend whom I will never forget.

FIRST ATTEMPT AT DISCHARGE

Time was passing by, and it was soon to be five years that I was committed.

Dr. Lee approached me in the hallway one day and said, "Ted, it's time to get you out of here. We have to go to the superintendence office for him to evaluate you for discharge. We will meet with him about a week."

The day came to see the superintendent. I walked over to Page Hall and went upstairs to his office. They called me into his office, where I sat at a table with the superintendent, Dr. Lee and Dr. Volkining.

The superintendent asked me to count backwards from a hundred by sevens. I counted till I was at thirty and I asked, "Should I keep going?" The answered, "Yes." When I was finished, he asked me a few more questions and then said I could leave.

It just happened that the day I was to go to court was the same day that our ward was to move to Merritt Hall. I brought all my belongings to the new ward but did not unpack; I was sure I would be discharged that day.

When I arrived at court, I was brought into a holding cell. I remember thinking that this would be the last time I'll have to be in a cell.

A short time later I was brought up to the courtroom.

The prosecutor called Dr. Lee to the stand first and asked him a number of questions, such as, what disorder did I have and what would happen if I was to stop taking my medications? Dr. Lee answered, "He is suffering from a disorder called chronic paranoid schizophrenia; without his medication he will become ill."

The prosecutor asked, "Without his medication would he become dangerous?" Dr. Lee answered, "There is no way of knowing except to stop his medication to see how he reacts."

They then called Dr. Volkining to stand. Once on the stand the prosecutor asked him the same question, he asked Dr. Lee; "What type of disorder does he have?" Dr. Volkining answer, "He has acute schizophrenia."

I didn't realize it then, but that answer cost me my release. Because it was the exact opposite of what Dr. Lee said. Needless to say, "I was denied my discharge."

MEDICATION DISCONTINUED

A couple of days later Dr. Volkining discontinued my medication. Now it would be a waiting game to see if I could rename stable off the medication.

Everything went well for the first several weeks. I went home to my mother's-on-Mother's Day weekend.

That Friday the day went well, and I fell asleep at about midnight. About six in the morning, I woke up out of a sound sleep, very paranoid. I was getting to the point where I was in and out of reality. I went upstairs and woke my mother. I told her she had to take me back to the hospital. I waited downstairs for her to come down and made her rush out of the house with me.

It seems like we drove forever and on the entire ride she kept saying to me, "Ted, you have to fight it. Just be the way you use to be."

By listening to her, I began to calm down and the paranoia went away.

We pulled into a diner, I asked my mom, "Where are we?" She answered, "Were in Massachusetts."

I hadn't his slightest idea that we drove that far. She got off the highway and turned back to Connecticut.

After we had returned home, I felt better than I have in years. (I didn't know then, but this euphoria was a warning sign.)

I was actually becoming more and more ill. I had just passed the point of no return; at this point, if you told me I was ill, I would not have believed you.

My sister's boyfriend was in the garage working on my sister's car. He came to me and asked, "Can a cracked distributor cap cause the engine to keep backfiring?"

I answered, "Yes, it can." I went out to the garage with him and showed him how to look for the crack.

Two hours later he came back in and said, "it's doing it again, even with the new distributor cap." I went back out with him and asked him, "Did you do anything since the last time?"

He said, "I changed the spark plug wires."

I checked the firing order and found that he crossed one of the wires. I switched the wires, and the car ran fine.

Later that Friday afternoon I drove my sister-in-law and her sister to work; they both worked at the same restaurant.

On the way there we were on the highway, and I saw a state police car on the highway in front of us. I caught up to him and drove right on his back bumper; then I passed him and pulled right in front of him.

He turned on his lights and pulled me over. He walked up to my car and said, "You know that wasn't the right thing to do, don't you?"

I answered, "You knew I was there."

He said it again," You know that was wrong."

I answered, "Yes sir."

He didn't check my license or my registration. He just said, "GO!"

(Talking about God being with me, huh!)

My sister-in-law Betty had a sister named Kim, who was staying with her. I had a big crush on Kim and from time to time she would ask to use my car. I thought she felt the same way for me; although she had a boyfriend, I thought we could get together. Turns out she just wanted to use my car.

My mother picked them up from work that evening and the two of them and my brother Charlie was going out to Howard Johnson's to have a couple drinks. I asked if I could come along? They said yes.

On the way to the bar Kim and I sat in the back. I grabbed her hand to hold it; she pulled away and got very angry. Nothing else was said.

At the bar I drank beer after beer and felt nothing. Next thing I knew it was closing time. I was growing more and more delusional.

I woke up early the next morning and cooked eggs for my nephew's dog, Toby, and myself.

Toby was his dog, but I was sort of Toby's master.

Outside, my sister's boyfriend, John, was working on her car again.

He asked me, "Want to car continue to run when you pull off the negative battery cable?"

I pulled the negative cable off, the car shut off. Normally I would have known that this meant the alternator was bad.

John started the car again and I pulled the cable off again; this happened three times.

After the third time John finally said, "If you make me start this car one more time, I'm going to go crazy.

I went back in the house.

My brother Charlie had a softball game that afternoon; so, I went to watch.

When I got to the game, it had already started. I walked right out onto the outfield and was waving for them to continue with the game.

I walked around to where my brother was; he looked at me very strange.

Later, I learned that he told the other players that I had a bad experience in Vietnam.

He asked me, "Can you go to the store and buy me some juice?" He handed me a $20 bill and I left.

On the way to the store, I noticed I was low on gas. I came to a gas station, pulled up to the pumps and tried to pump gas. Then I realized the station was closed.

The funny thing was, other people saw me trying to pump gas and thought the station was open and pulled in to get gas too. They looked at me real strange; I drove away.

I could only find one store open. It was a gift store. I walked in, looked around; and realized I would not find anything to drink here.

Then for some reason I started to look around for Mother's Day gifts for my mother and grandmother. I found two gifts and walked up to the register. The woman rang up the gifts and it came to $25. I said, "I only have $20." The woman said, "That would be enough." She was a very nice woman.

I drove back to the field; told Charlie there were no stores open that sold juice. He asked, "Where's the 20?" I said, "I spent it." He just looked at me and shook his head. I returned home.

Later that night I couldn't sleep so I decided to take Toby for a ride. As I was about to get into the car my mother called down from the window, she said, Ted! You are going to run out of gas. I said nothing and got in the car with Tobby.

We drove for a while and came to a gas station; I went to the tellers' window and asked, "Can I have some gas?" The teller said, "No." I got back in the car and drove onto the highway. Less than a mile I ran out of gas; I pulled over to the side and parked.

I slept the night in the car. Early in the morning my mother pulled up in back of me; she told me to get the dog and get in the car.

I asked, "How did you find me?" She answered, "Charlie went by you on his way to work and called me."

We returned home and had some coffee; then it was time to return to the hospital.

When we arrived, we walked into the supervisors office. My mom asked the supervisor, "Can we speak to Dr. Volkining, it's very important?" She sent us down to his office.

Inside his office he asked us to take a seat. My mom looked at me. I told her, "Tell him whatever you want to tell him."

She told him everything that happened over the weekend. When she finished, he said, "We will have to put him back on his medication to stabilize him, I have never seen him like this."

When I was brought onto my ward, I knew something was very different. All the beds were stripped of linen and the lockers were all open.

This was just what my mind needs to see. I started to jump to conclusions, like, all these patients are not really patients bought, rather, they are here to protect me and now there is no danger, so we are all going home.

I walked into the day room where they were having a meeting. They were just ending when I walked in, so I did not know what is really going on at this point.

At that moment I decided to quit smoking and asked if anyone wanted my cigarettes? They all did.

Then Tony, the staff member, asked me to go into the reading room for a minute.

He then asked, "Ted, are you okay?" I answered, "Yes, why?" He said, "You are laughing at things that are not funny." I said, "I'm okay, Tony." He said, "Okay."

I went and sat down in the smoking room. I was there for about 10 minutes when Jane came in with a cup of medication and said, "Ted, take this so you will feel better." I answered, "I'm not taking that, you take it!"

She walked out of the room. About five minutes later she came in and asked, "Can you come down to your room?"

I got up and went to my room. Inside the room was my psychologist, and Kathy the head nurse, and two guys that were twice my size. They asked again, "Take the medication." Again, I refused. The next thing I knew, I was on the bed with one of the guy's knees in my bad shoulder and I heard it crack; he then choked me until I passed out. They then put me in a straitjacket.

They laid me on the bed, which I didn't mind, but when they took my shoes off, I felt very humiliated.

They said, "You should feel better by tomorrow."

A short while later Tony came in and asked, "Can I get you something?" I said, "I'm okay, Tony." He said, "I wish I had not gone to lunch at that time. Maybe I could have prevented this." He then took off to straitjacket. I said, "Thank you."

As I lay there, I was having racing thoughts; I thought that my watch had a bomb in it, so I threw it on to my till.

I also thought that the patient across the room was going to rape me.

I walked out into the day room and said to Tony, "My grandmother is very ill, and I have to go to her. (None of this was true except in my mind). Tony said, "If she is in any danger someone will call to let us know."

I asked, "Can you buy me a pack of cigarettes?" He said, "I can do that. Let's take a walk to the canteen." In the canteen my cigarettes were sold out on my brand. He said, "By the nearest one to your brand." I said," Thank you." And we went back to the ward.

I had a cigarette and went straight back to my room. It did not take me long to fall asleep.

The next morning when I woke up, I was having a great deal of pain in my left shoulder, where the goon put his knee into my shoulder. I went to the office and by chance the medical doctor was in there. I told him that once I had a bone graft to my left shoulder and that I thought it was broken. He pressed on my shoulder, and I could feel the bone moving. He said sarcastically, "What do you know, it moves. It will heal on its own."

Kathy then evaluated me and decided to give me my privileges back.

About a month later I had gotten off of work and was sitting outside of Battell on a bench. Another man, a visitor, sat down next to me, he said, "You're the guy who murdered his wife! Aren't you? If I was your brother-law I would plant, you under the flower bed." I said, "Well, you're not my brother-in-law, but if you would like to try to plant me, then go ahead and try!" He said, "I'm a Viet Nam Vet." I said, "Do you think you are the only vet?" He looked at me and said, "She was probably the only person that loved you." That hit home and I just got up and said, "You are probably right about that." I walked away.

I could go on about the things that happened the next two years, but there is nothing really interesting.

Two years later I walked into Dr. Volkining in the hall; I stopped him and asked him, "if he thought it was time to go back to court. "He replied, "it is time, I will contact the court and arrange a hearing."

A couple of weeks later a date of September 15, 1983, was set. In about two weeks I would try to be discharged again.

The wait passed; it was the morning of September 15. The sheriffs arrived at 9 AM.

We arrived at the courthouse, and I was brought to the holding cell. When inside I thought, this may be the last time that I will have to sit in a cell.

I was only waiting about 20 minutes when the public defender came down to the cell and took me upstairs to his office. He said, "Take a seat, you should have been released two years ago. I'm going to get you out of here today; so, don't be nervous, we will be through in less than an hour."

There were only two other people inside the court, my mother and my sister.

The judge came into the room, and we got started. The judge said to my attorney, "You won the last three cases this morning; let the other side win one." My attorney replied, "Not a chance Your Honor.

Dr. Volkining was the only one to testify. The prosecutor asked him, "Would I be able to take and maintain my own medication?" The doctor replied, "He is well aware of the importance of taking his medication."

That was the only question the prosecutor asked.

My attorney said to the judge, "The superintendent of the hospital also agrees that Mr. LaPointe does not present a danger to himself or others." The judge said to me, "You have been up there a long time. I'm going to release you to the custody of your mother, and you are to be placed on probation not to exceed 25 years. You may now leave."

I was free!

Little did I know then that I would be back at the hospital in four years.

The previous sentence is where this books original draft ends. As you can see there is little to no hope in this ending. But thank God: the story isn't finished!

I would like to write about Patty. She was a faithful and devoted wife, unlike myself at being a husband, who had forgiven me of many wrongs, including, committing adultery three times.

Twice in our marriage we were without our own place to live. The longest job I held down was one year. Our children always had on clean clothes and our home was always neat. I could not have asked for a better wife.

When I first met Patty; I could not go a day without being with her. She was all I thought about. We were extremely happy.

So how could a man who was drafted into the United States Marine Corps a few years before, whom never had a problem holding down a job before then, come home with an honorable discharge and not be able to sustain employment?

Then, this man marries the wife of his dreams and in less than four years commits adultery three different times. Also, this man's alcohol and drug abuse went out of control.

Then, four years later, this man shoots and kills his wife and shoots himself but, by the grace of God he was able to survive!

I am told that it is the schizophrenia; I can attest to the fact that schizophrenia is one of the most debilitating diseases I know. It goes hand in hand with the enemy of our souls, who only comes to steal, kill and destroy.!

For me each episode I had had an insidious onset; each one began with the experience of euphoria. Little by little I lost contact with reality until I was in a world of fantasy and lies. Paranoia, or a better word may be terror; fear so frightening that it can't be put into words; where there is no escape from it; no place to hide. A place where you do not trust anyone.

I have been blessed that each episode after the first I have had people in my life to intervene and get me the help I've needed. I thank them all.

Schizophrenia had taken everything in my life that I loved. Today, at least at this time, I do not have my children in my life. They have been told all their lives that I was no good and that I planed the shooting. They hold unforgiveness and resentment for the sins I have committed in my life. I am not bitter, and I understand how they feel. The world feels these kinds of things.

I am blessed to have been lifted to a higher realm. I hold no resentment towards anyone, including myself.

Today I am 70 years of age. I have lived in the same apartment for nine years. I have a nice vehicle; I am financially stable and am able to be a blessing to others; I believe that is what it is all about. To love your neighbor as yourself.

Thank you for reading my story. God Bless.

www.ingramcontent.com/pod-product-compliance
Lightning Source LLC
Chambersburg PA
CBHW070711130626
46553CB00005B/1943